# CRACKER HORSES AND CATTLE

## A HISTORY OF FLORIDA'S HERITAGE BREEDS

**CAROL MATTHEWS**

THE
History
PRESS

Published by The History Press
Charleston, SC
www.historypress.com

First published 2023

Manufactured in the United States

ISBN 9781467151009

Library of Congress Control Number: 2023938573

# CONTENTS

CONTENTS

# ACKNOWLEDGMENTS

I owe a debt of gratitude to so many people for answering my questions and requests for photographs over the past five years. First, thank you to my husband, Jack Gillen, for being a living example of Florida's history. His wealth of knowledge and collection of archives from the Florida Cracker Horse and Cattle Associations provided materials that make this book unique among others, and I am grateful for his patience and expert editing. Thank you to the Florida Cattlemen's Foundation and Florida Cattlemen's Association for their permission to reprint the biographies and photographs of noted Floridians in the cattle business; Bob Stone for his photographs and stories; Stephen Monroe and Dr. Tim Olsen for their photographs of Cracker horses and Cracker cattle; to Doyle Conner Jr. for his commitment to preserving Florida's history ("He ain't no sissie!"); Robbie Adams from Adams Ranch for taking time out of his busy life to send me family photographs; Iris Wall for providing research material on Florida's history from her extensive library and for her patience with my countless questions over the years; Impact Computers of Gainesville without whose help this book would never have gone to print; to judge and storyteller Nelson Bailey for his stories; and to all those who provided comments and photographs from their experience on the Great Florida Cattle Drive. My apologies if your photograph or comments did not appear in the final copy. I will hold you all and those experiences in my heart forever!

# INTRODUCTION

I will always remember the day I met two influential women who have left an indelible mark on Florida's history. One was a Seminole Indian. One was a Florida Cracker. Both were born in the same small village of Indiantown, Florida, and both were lifelong friends. Their names were Betty Mae Tiger Jumper and Iris Pollock Wall. Betty Mae was the only female leader of the Seminole tribe of Florida, and Iris became Woman of the Year in Agriculture for the State of Florida. Both women were together this day, commemorating Seminole women in the cattle industry. Seminoles are matrilineal, and as such, women own their own cattle. I had heard of these women, having recently gained a second grade teaching position in Indiantown, but I had not had the privilege of meeting them. But here they were, together on the same day.

I had seen a flier advertising a ceremonial cattle drive in the Big Cypress Reservation in South Florida. Having been born in Ohio and raised by a farmer, I know the attraction that working with animals has for many people. I missed my farm girl background, I guess, and knew little about Seminole history, so I decided to go. When the drive stopped for lunch under a big tent, there was storytelling. Afterward, I introduced myself, thanked the two women for their stories and came away with a promise that Iris would come and speak to my class. As it turned out, Iris still lived in Indiantown and had previously attended Warfield School, where I now taught. That day was the beginning of the "living history" lessons about Florida history that I would learn and later write about. They came from a woman who would become my friend, my "other" mother and my favorite teacher, Iris Wall, a Florida Cracker cowgirl.

That day launched my desire to learn more about Florida's cow culture, the history of horses and cattle in Florida. Most people think the Indians out west always had horses. But as I learned, it was Florida that was the first territory to have the horse. It was Florida that was the first territory to have the cow. Thankfully, people took steps to save these breeds, and they are now known as Florida's heritage animals, Florida's Cracker horses and Cracker cattle. They both may be the oldest breeds in North America, according to the Florida Cracker Horse and Cracker Cattle Associations, with the newest registry.

Some wonderful books have already been written about the histories of these animals and the culture they produced. Most notable are *A Land Remembered*, by Patrick Smith (adult and children's versions); *Florida Cattle Ranching: Five Centuries of Tradition*, by the Florida Cattlemen's Foundation; and *Florida Cowboys: Keepers of the Last Frontier*, by Carlton Ward Jr. My mission is to add to that number and perhaps inspire people to learn more about Florida's agricultural history. My hope is that they take action to continue to preserve and protect the state's agricultural lands, heritage animals and native species and their habitats.

I laugh when I wear my "Cracker Cattle Association" cap into the grocery store, because frequently, someone will ask, "What is a Cracker cow?" And then I'll launch into my condensed version of their history. I always think, if these questions come from Floridians, imagine what other folks don't know. Hopefully, readers will come away with a little more knowledge about America's first horses and cattle, where they came from, who tended them for the past five hundred years and who protects and celebrates their history today.

*Proceeds from this book will go toward the preservation of Florida's Cracker Horses and Cattle through continued efforts to educate the public about the history of their breeds.*

# A HISTORY OF AMERICA'S FIRST HORSES AND CATTLE

*Of all the events that shaped the history of our continent, the arrival of the first horses and cattle remains unequaled in its significance. Before there was a Wild West, there was a Wild Florida, with cattle drives, cowboys, saloons, gun fights and new homesteads. Even most present-day Florida residents are not aware of the part horses and cattle played in the state's history; and the part they still play. Not many tourists are drawn to the flat prairies which fill the vast area between the Atlantic and Gulf Coast beaches; and between Disney World and the Everglades most people focus mostly on Lake Okeechobee and fishing. But scenes reminiscent of Old Florida can still be found. One thing that keeps Florida ranches anchored to the past is that horses have not been replaced by four-wheel-drive vehicles as much as in the West. Marshes, swamps, ponds, rivers, hammocks and water-control ditches are still traversed better by "four hooves" than "four wheels" in many cases.*
*—Florida Cracker Horse Association archives*

## THE SPANISH VAQUEROS

Prehistoric horses disappeared long ago in North America. Norsemen were thought to have sailed west around the year 1000 BC and were said to have brought dairy and beef cattle with them when they reached the shores of Iceland and Greenland. Though the Norsemen's stories are still studied by notable scholars, there is no supported documentation of these adventures, as the Norsemen left no traceable records.

In 1492, Spanish explorer Cristóbal Colón, who later called himself Christopher Columbus, made a successful first voyage to a Caribbean island he named Española, or "Little Spain," where he built the fortress of La Navidad. He sailed back to Spain exactly one year later to share the news of his discovery and gain permission from the Spanish Crown to establish a colony in Española.

According to author Deb Bennett, PhD, in a royal decree made in Barcelona on May 23, 1493, King Ferdinand and Queen Isabella stated, "Among the persons which we order to go in the armada to the New World, we have agreed that twenty lancers are to sail with horses. Therefore, we mandate that from among the persons of the Holy Brotherhood living in this Kingdom of Granada, twenty horsemen should be selected. Five of them shall bring spare horses, and those spare horses shall be mares." This would indicate that the Spanish sovereigns intended on initiating the practice of horse breeding, further stating that "if the boats do not have sufficient capacity, it is permitted to throw out some things so that the horses might go." Columbus had a choice to make concerning what kind of horses to bring to the Americas, wrote Nelson E. Bailey in *Florida's "Little" Horses: A Little Amble Through Florida History*.

*For there were small Spanish riding horses, and large Spanish riding horses and the two kinds served different purposes. In Spain, military horsemen of his day had one of each kind: a small, gaited marching horse for traveling cross-country; and a large, trotting "war" horse for going into battle. Each military horseman mounted his taller horse only for mounted games or military practice, and, most importantly, immediately before going into combat. This before-the-battle switch from a short marching horse to a tall war horse was a ritual. We still use a phrase that refers to it whenever someone starts to get verbally combative with us. We say something like "Why are you getting on your high horse?" Columbus chooses to bring the pony-sized marching horses, which under the circumstances seemed like a sound decision. The smaller horses were easier to transport and a larger number would fit in the space allowed. Horses in the New World were needed primarily for travel rather than fighting. Even if fighting with the native population were to become necessary, it was learned on an earlier voyage that the native inhabitants did not possess horses.*

Columbus returned to Hispaniola, this time with horses and cattle, sheep, swine and other livestock, along with permission to establish a new colony.

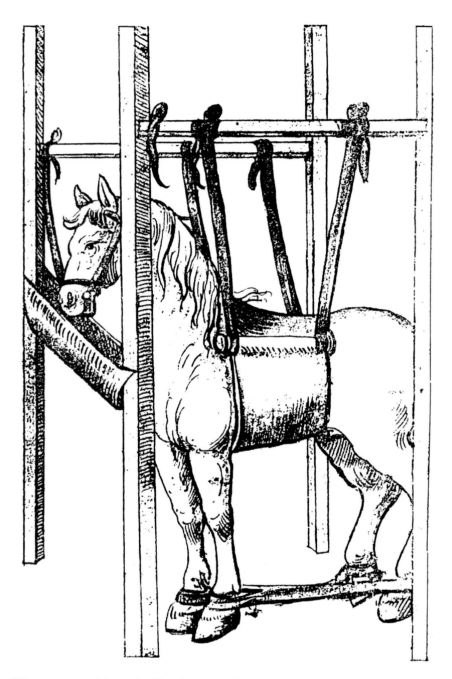

"Thus one suspends horses in ships when one wishes to send them across the sea."
*Christopher Weiditz (circa 1500–1550) in Das trachtenbuch der C. Weiditz; Library of Congress.*

It is not known how many horses disembarked from his ship with the other livestock. Some historians place the number at a few more than thirty, while others have spoken of a greater number. After landing, the horses were lowered from the sailing vessels and were said to have been able to walk off the ships, be mounted and break trail while carrying almost one-quarter their weight. After being forced to hang in slings, with rations of stale hay and small quantities of water, certainly only horses and cattle of superior breeding could have endured the rough sea crossing.

From the perspective of a Native inhabitant watching the horses embark from the ship, author Dr. Deb Bennett described the horses:

*They had eyes like the eyes of men, and voices like the voice of the hurricane. Their tonic smell, wafting like a high harmonic above the foul odor of the bilge, struck his nostrils like acid. He snorted. They snorted. Slung by belly bands within open-sided crates erected to support and confine them on deck, they moved their hammer-feel uneasily, extended their long and handsomely fringed red necks, rolled their eyes, and snapped their white teeth.*

The Native inhabitants of the island were initially awestruck and assumed subservient roles to the mounted Spanish explorers. This greatly assisted the Spanish quest for land and gold.

No part of the island of Espanola originally had horses or cattle; new herds were bred from the very first stock brought from Spain. The Caribbean's perfect climate and lack of parasites and predators at this time led to a vast increase in the horse and cattle population. Horse breeding and cattle ranching expanded across Hispaniola (the Dominican Republic and Haiti, as the areas later became known) and into Cuba and Puerto Rico; it then expanded into North, Central and South America. As adventurers continued to explore and colonize new lands, they took livestock from this central location with them.

These early horses, like the cattle, were the products of selective breeding and were descendants of the sixteenth-century Spanish jennet, a type of horse then bred in the provinces of Extremadura and Andalusia, Spain, writes Deb Bennett, PhD, in *Conquerors: The Roots of New World Horsemanship*. Spanish horses roamed Andalusia before the Romans reached the Iberian Peninsula. The significance and beauty of the Spanish jenet is well depicted in early Roman art, including mosaics, paintings and sculptures. These horses were not only beautiful, but they were also nimble and ferocious in war, so much so that the leading historian of the time, Saint Isidor of

Seville, declared Iberian horses "the best in the world." Unmatched in intelligence, endurance and speed, they were descended from the Arabian and Barb stock brought to Spain by the Moors, mixed with additional bloodlines from the Norse dun. So prized were they that European royalty favored them exclusively. French kings, from Francis to Louis XIV, rode Spanish/Iberian mounts.

In 1493, explorer Juan Ponce de León sailed with Christopher Columbus on his second voyage to the New World. He had been a soldier who fought for the Spanish Crown against the Moors in Granada, and his wealth and success as a soldier gave him the status to join Columbus. In 1508, Ponce de León was granted permission from the Crown to colonize Puerto Rico and was given the title of governor. He sailed to Puerto Rico and formed a settlement. After the death of Christopher Columbus, Columbus's son Diego began pressuring the Spanish Crown to grant him his inheritance and replaced Ponce de León as governor of Puerto Rico. Restless to pursue his dream of finding land of his own, Ponce de León set out again to explore the island of Bimini for presumed riches and to find the Fountain of Youth, a stream the Taino Indians told him could make an old person young again after drinking from its magical waters. (This was most likely a story created to get Ponce de León off the island.) Although he failed to discover the Fountain of Youth, Ponce de León did discover a peninsula on Eastertide in 1513. He named this land, lush with flowers, longleaf pine, mangrove swamps and cypress forests, La Florida, or "the land of flowers."

Ponce de León set sail for Florida once again in 1521, twenty-nine years after Columbus's first voyage. After coming ashore near what is now Estero Bay, close to present-day Tampa on the Gulf Coast, Ponce de León brought soldiers, settlers, seeds and tools, along with fifty horses and a small herd of black Andalusian cattle and other livestock, with the

An artist's rendering of Juan Ponce de León, the Spanish explorer who made the first recorded landing of a white man in Florida on April 2, 1513, near St. Augustine. *Florida Archives.*

intention of establishing a colony. These were the first horses and the first cattle ever recorded as setting hoof on the shores of what is now the continental United States. This was nineteen years before the Spanish explorer Francisco Vázquez de Coronado brought the first horses to the American Southwest from Mexico in his search for the City of Gold and ninety-nine years before the Pilgrims landed in New England.

Ponce de León and his crew were attacked by the Calusa Indians. They were forced back on their ship, which they sailed back to Cuba, where Ponce de León later died of a wound caused by a poison arrow. In the explorers' haste to escape, they left their livestock behind. It is not known what became of the animals, but it can be assumed they were the first horses and cattle to ever run wild in Florida.

Ponce de León was soon followed by other conquistadors, who brought livestock with the intentions of establishing colonies in Florida. In 1539, Hernando de Soto led a host of Iberian knights through Florida in search of gold. He brought cattle, swine and many horses, along with dogs for herding stock and tracking Indians. He later reported seeing native bison in the northern regions of the state.

In 1540, Don Diego Maldonado was sent to resupply De Soto's depleted resources. Maldonado brought a large herd of cattle to Santa Rosa County but was unable to reach De Soto's expedition, so many of the cattle were lost or left with the Indians. When these early attempts to establish a colony failed, the livestock were repeatedly left to roam free. Over time, these horses and cattle established themselves in wild herds, adapting to the hot, wet, insect-infested areas of Florida. And after many generations, they began to thrive and multiply and become a part of Florida's woodlands and prairies, where, previously, only deer and bison had grazed.

In 1565, Pedro Menéndez de Avilés founded St. Augustine, and it became the first permanently occupied city in the New World. Even though Pedro Menéndez de Avilés brought "two hundred heifer calves" from Spanish stock to supply the new colony, by 1570, St. Augustine faced a food shortage. In addition to the colony's sandy soil not being conducive to growing vegetables, one visitor observed, "Their cattle were being devoured by mosquitos or killed by Indians, and there remained but ten or twelve cows and fifteen or sixteen mares." It was 1605 before the first working rancho, or Spanish ranch, started operations, but within a few years, these Spanish ranches were scattered over much of the northern part of the state. The Jesuit and Franciscan friars who worked to Christianize the Indians discovered that these Indians were quite skilled at working cattle and taming the spirited

14

Old Spanish brands drawn by Joe Ackerman. *Florida Archives.*

Spanish horses to ride. Though Spanish tax reports were commonly falsified and the number of cattle kept by the Indians unknown, it is estimated that the number of cattle in Florida in 1700 could have totaled six thousand.

The main ranching areas during periods of Spanish colonization (1565–1763, 1783–1819) were Paynes Prairie in Alachua County, Tallahassee–St. Marks, inland from St. Augustine along the St. John's River and, later, Pensacola. By 1618, Florida's Spanish governors were making greater efforts to increase beef production, and by 1640, breeding stock was being imported from Cuba to build up the herds. Although there was still a shortage of beef in some areas, rancheros, or Spanish ranchers, began selling cattle back to Cuba illegally, because they could make a larger profit due to Spain's attempt to regulate cattle prices in the New World. This practice established a commercial tie with Cuba that would continue for hundreds of years, and it became the first industry in the New World.

In 1698, Spanish tax rolls listed thirty-four ranchos stretching from the St. Johns valley to Apalachicola. The largest cattle operation, Rancho de la Chua (later Alachua), was established by Francisco Menéndez Márquez around 1637. The rancho was located in an area of lush grasses and rich soil, known today as Paynes Prairie. There may have been as many as one thousand head of cattle on this Spanish ranch. Because the range land was so extensive and many areas were difficult to traverse, an accurate number of cattle was difficult to establish, but some records give numbers as high as fifteen thousand to twenty thousand head of cattle. Florida looked promising as an economic investment for the Spanish Crown during this time. But with the establishment of Charles Town (later Charleston) by the British in 1639, this changed.

News of the existence of these vast herds of cattle eventually spread, and British bandits from South Carolina began raiding and stealing cattle from the Franciscan missions. When war broke out in Europe between Britain and Spain, British governor Colonel James Moore of South Carolina sent troops, along with a band of Oconee Indians, into Florida to destroy Spanish settlements. Some 1,500 of Moore's men raided and burned years of Spanish criolla tradition by butchering or driving off 6,000 cattle and capturing or killing 7,000 Indians. When they left Rancho de la Chua, all that was left were cattle that had been scattered into the area's piney woods and prairies.

Moore's men turned next toward Fort Castillo de San Marcos. They were unable to destroy the community due to efforts from the citizens of St. Augustine, who drove livestock into their large fort compound, which enabled them to have sufficient food to survive the attack. Moore's troops were unable to completely destroy the Spanish mission settlements, but years would pass before the herds were able to be replenished. Though Spanish rule dominated Florida for over two hundred years, little of Spanish influence lasted. What did endure was something that was arguably more valuable in the long run than gold—the foundation herds of Spanish cattle and horses that supplied stock for some of the first ranches in Florida that remain today.

## SEMINOLE COW KEEPERS

Among the Oconee Indians who accompanied the British troops who raided Florida was an Oconee Creek leader named Ahaya, later known as Cowkeeper. After assisting Col Moore's raid on the Spanish ranches, Ahaya returned to South Carolina, where he gathered his people and brought them back to Florida to an area known as Cuscowilla, just south of Rancho de la Chua. This would become the first settlement of the Seminole people, referring to several tribes of Florida Indians who separated from the Creeks. Cowkeeper would become the first leader and forefather of the Seminole tribe. Paynes Prairie, just to the north, was named after Cowkeeper's nephew Payne. Payne's nephew was Micanopy. A town of the same name would later appear, and it now sits on the ancient remains of Cuscowilla. Micanopy's nephew was Billy Bowlegs. All of these men became famous leaders of the Seminole tribe.

Cowkeeper and his relatives gathered up the abandoned, scattered Spanish cattle and horses near La Chua and, over time, established large herds near the Paynes Prairie area. Grazing on Paynes Prairie in 1775 were seven to ten thousand head of cattle, according to one historian. Adopting the Spanish style, the Seminoles used dogs and Spanish horses to herd cattle. They called the cattle *waki(t)*, after the Spanish word *vaca*, and the horses *kawayi* after the Spanish word

Micanopy, the head "Micco" of all the Seminole chiefs. *Florida Archives.*

*caballo.* Slavery was a long-held practice among the southeastern Indians, and Black slaves fleeing to Florida from southern plantations gave the Seminoles added manpower to tend their cattle. Although the Seminoles owned cattle and other livestock, they did not understand the concept of owning land individually. They always used the range land communally, and this basic cultural difference led to later conflict among the southern plantation owners and early American cattlemen.

In 1791, William Bartram, an American botanist and nature explorer, was described as the first naturalist who traversed the dense forests of Florida. During one particular expedition to Florida, when Bartram traveled with members of a trading company destined to establish trading with Cowkeeper and other chiefs of Cuscowilla, he described his arrival:

*We were welcomed to the town, and conducted by the young men and maidens to the chief's house, which stood on an eminence, and was distinguished from the rest by its superior magnitude, a large flag being hoisted on a high staff at one corner. We immediately alighted: the chief, who is called the Cowkeeper, attended by several ancient men, came to us, and in a very free and sociable manner shook our hands, or rather arms, (a form of salutation peculiar to the American Indians) saying at the same time, "You are come." We followed him to an apartment prepared for the reception of their guests.*

*The pipe being filled, it is handed around; after which a large bowl, with what they call "thin drink," is brought in and set down on a small low table. In this bowl is a great wooden ladle; each person takes up in it as he pleases, and after drinking until satisfied, returns it again into the bowl, pushing the handle towards the next person in the circle; and so it goes round.*

*The chief is a tall well made man, very affable and cheerful, about sixty years of age, his eyes lively and full of fire, his countenance manly and placid, yet ferocious, or what we call savage, his nose aquiline, his dress extremely simple, but his head ornamented in the true Creek mode.*

*After the usual compliments and inquiries relative to our adventures &c. the chief trader informed the Cowkeeper, in the presence of his council or attendants, the purport of our business, with which he expressed his satisfaction. He was then informed what the nature of my errand was, and he received me with complaisance, giving me unlimited permission to travel over the country for the purpose of collecting flowers, medicinal plants, &c. saluting me by the name of Puc Puggy, or the Flower Hunter, recommending me to the friendship and protection of his people. The repast is now brought in, consisting of venison, stewed with bear's oil, fresh corn cakes, milk, and hominy; and our drink, honey and water, very cool and agreeable. After partaking of this banquet, we took leave and departed for the great savanna.*

*The extensive Alachua savanna is a level green plain, above fifteen miles over, fifty miles in circumference, and scarcely a tree or bush of any kind to be seen on it. It is encircled with high, sloping hills, covered with waving forests, and fragrant orange groves, rising from an exuberantly fertile soil. The towering magnolia grandiflora and transcendent palm stand conspicuous amongst them. At the same time are seen innumerable droves of cattle; the lordly bull, lowing cow, and sleek capricious heifer. The hills and groves re-echo their cheerful, social voices. Herds of sprightly deer, squadrons of the beautiful fleet Siminole [sic] horse, flocks of turkeys, civilized communities of the sonorous watchful crane, mix together, appearing happy and contented in the enjoyment of peace, till disturbed and affrighted by the warrior man.*

*Behold yonder, coming upon them through the darkened groves, sneakingly and unawares, the naked red warrior. At the terrible appearance of the painted, fearless, uncontrolled and free Siminole [sic], the peaceful innocent nations are at once thrown into disorder and dismay. The red warrior, whose plumed head flashes lightning, whoop in vain; his proud ambitious horse strains and pants; the earth glides from under his feet, his flowing mane whistles in the wind, as he comes up full of vein hopes. The bounding roe views his rapid approaches, rises up, lifts loft his antlered head, erects the white flag [alluding to his tail], and fetching a shrill whistle, says to his fleet and free associates, "follow"; he bounds off, and in a few minutes distances his foe a mile.*

*We approached the savanna at the south end by a narrow isthmus of level ground. This isthmus being the common avenue or road of Indian travelers, we pitched our camp at a small distance from it, on a rising knoll near the verge of the savanna, under some spreading Live Oaks....Soon after sunrise, a party of Indians on horseback appeared upon the savanna, to collect together several herds of cattle which they drove along near our camp, towards the town. One of the party came up, and informed us, that the cattle belonged to the Chief of Cuscowilla; that he had ordered some of the best steers of his droves to be slaughtered for a general feast for the whole town, in compliment of our arrival, and pacific negotiations.*

*The cattle were as large and fat as those of the rich grazing pastures of Moyomensing in Pennsylvania. The Indians drove off the lowing herds, and we soon followed them to town, in order to be at council at the appointed hour, leaving two young men of our party to protect our camp.*

*Upon our arrival we repaired to the public square or council-house, where the chiefs and senators were already convened; the warriors and young men assembled soon after, the business being transacted in public. As it was no more than a ratification of the late treaty of St. Augustine, with some particular commercial stipulations, with respect to the citizens of Alachua, the negotiations soon terminated to the satisfaction of both parties.*

*The banquet succeeded; the ribs and choicest fat pieces of the bullocks, excellently well barbecued, were brought into the apartment of the public square, constructed and appointed for feasting; bowls and kettles of stewed flesh and broth were brought in for feasting; next course, and with it a very singular dish, the traders call it cleaned of its contents, cut and minced pretty fine, and then made the seasoning not quite strong enough to extinguish its original flavour and scent. This dish is greatly esteemed by the Indians, but is, in my judgment, the least agreeable they have amongst them.*

*After the feast was over, we returned to our encampment on the great savanna, towards evening. The next morning cool and pleasant, and the skies serene, we decamped, pursuing our progress round the Alachua savanna. Our progress this day was extremely pleasant, over the green turf, having in view numerous herds of cattle and deer, and squadrons of horse peacefully browsing on the tender, sweet grass, or strolling through the cool fragrant groves on the surrounding heights.*

*Passing through a great extent of ancient Indian fields, now grown over with forests of stately trees, orange groves and luxuriant herbage, the old trader, my associate, informed me it was the ancient Alachua, the capital of that famous and powerful tribe, who peopled the hills surrounding the savanna, when, in days of old, they could assemble by thousands at ball play and other juvenile diversions and athletic exercises, over those, then happy, fields and green plains. And there is no reason for me to doubt his account being true, as almost every step we take over those fertile heights, discovers remains and traces of ancient human habitations and cultivations.*

Eventually, Cowkeeper's nephew Payne of Paynes Prairie became the leader of the Alachua band of Seminoles, and the wealth of the tribe continued to grow. Raising cattle was no longer just a source of food, but it was also a means to acquire money. Conflict arose on the Florida-Georgia border. Cattle from both sides wandered, and both stole cattle from each other. This animosity would eventually lead to three Seminole Wars.

In 1817, Andrew Jackson was sent to Florida by the U.S. Department of War with over three thousand troops comprising Tennessee volunteers, U.S. regulars and Creek Indians. The major settlements of Tallahassee, Miccosukee and Alachua were burned. This action would later become known as the First Seminole War.

Florida became a territory in 1821, and in 1823, the U.S. Supreme Court made a decision that Indians could occupy lands within the United States but could not hold title to the land because their right of occupancy was subordinate to the United States' right of discovery. During this time, some of the main cattle ranching settlers came to the Alachua area, and competition for grazing rights became a constant source of tension between settlers and Indians. The Treaty of Fort Moultrie Creek tried to force the Seminoles to an inland reservation. Many Seminoles moved south, taking with them whatever supplies and cattle they could, but they were cut off from the ocean and not able to trade with Cuba. They also did not have the benefit of their crop season and nearly starved to death. Some Seminoles managed to keep their cattle along the Apalachicola River.

With the forthcoming Indian Removal Act, which came on May 26, 1830, the Seminoles were forced to give up their land in Florida and offered land in Oklahoma. They were promised cattle in Oklahoma equal to the numbers of cattle they left behind in Florida and cash for their cattle, but the promised cattle were of lesser value, and the cash was not sufficient for their survival. These conditions led to the costliest Indian war in the history of the United States, the Second Seminole War. Led by Seminole war leaders Osceola, Black Dirt, Alligator, Jumper and Abiaka, the Seminoles refused to acknowledge the treaty, and conflict ensued.

Despite cattle rustling and disagreements over grazing rights, the persistent Seminole cattlemen continued to amass large herds, grazing them in the excellent pastures around south Florida's Lake Okeechobee, Big Cypress and Fish Eating Creek. However, conflicts continued with the ever-increasing number of white settlers moving southward with their need for fertile pasture lands, and this conflict led to the Third Seminole War. The American government continued its efforts to force the Seminoles to give up their land.

In 1852, Seminole leader Billy Bowlegs was taken on a tour of Washington, D.C.; Boston; and New York City. He was interviewed by a reporter from a New Orleans newspaper, the *Daily Delta*, and Bowlegs reportedly told him, "I saw the Great Father in the White House [Millard Fillmore]. I told him that no one could scare me from Florida; if I wanted to go, I would; if I did not,

Chief Osceola. *Florida Archives.*

I would not." It was reported that some two hundred Seminoles were all who endured by the end of the Seminole Wars. But with the aid of their superior horses, guerrilla warfare tactics and their ability to adapt to the challenging Florida climate, a few Seminoles survived.

Since the question of cattle and range rights had been one of the principal causes of the wars, those remaining Indians vowed not to raise cattle again, although they did continue to raise hogs. So, it was not until the twentieth century that the Florida Seminoles went back to cattle ranching.

Because of the Seminoles' knowledge of moving cattle through Florida's rough terrain, they were critical to the efforts of supplying food to both the Confederate and Union troops during the Civil War. The Union army had cut off all supplies of beef except those from Florida. Florida ranchers contracted with the Seminoles to provide guidance and protection from the Union soldiers as they traveled with the "Cow Cavalry" on their cattle drives, leading herds up to Orlando and the Gulf Coast.

After the Civil War, Seminoles again tried to raise cattle around the Lake Okeechobee area, but their efforts were hindered by constant threat of rustlers. Eventually, by the beginning of the twentieth century, they had established herds around the Brighton and Big Cypress Reservations. In 1937, a successful cattle management program took hold after three decades of leadership by agricultural agent Fred Monstedeoca and the help of five Seminole men who had previously worked with cattle. Frank Shore, Charlie Micco, Naha Tiger, Willie Gopher and Willie Tiger became the first modern Seminole cattlemen.

Today, according to records maintained by the Ah-Tah-Thi-Ki Museum, located on the Seminole tribe of Florida's Big Cypress Reservation, the number of cattle at Brighton and Big Cypress is estimated to be around twenty thousand, all maintained on 90,372 acres of tribally owned land, making the Seminole tribe one of the leading beef producers in the United States. This was one of the first ranches to implement and test a national program that allows the U.S. Department of Agriculture to track the health

*Left*: Seminole Indian cowboy Charlie Micco and his grandson Fred Smith, Brighton Reservation 1950. Charlie Micco helped establish the cattle management program when the U.S. government shipped a starter herd of starving Hereford cattle from the Dust Bowl states to the Brighton Reservation in 1936. Fred Smith became president of the Seminole Tribe in 1971. *Florida Archives.*

*Right:* Justin Gopher with a Cracker horse, Big Cypress Indian Reservation, July 2007, takes a break during the annual roundup. The small agile horses descended from stock left by the Spanish in the sixteenth century make exceptional ranch horses. *Florida Archives.*

and locations of animals marked for human consumption. The program identifies a cow from birth and tracks it throughout its entire life, which can help monitor and control potential threats of disease, as described in *Florida Cattle Ranching, Five Centuries of Tradition, Florida Cattleman's Foundation.*

In the twenty-first century, Florida Seminole Alex Johns served alongside other Florida cattlemen in the office of the president of the Florida Cattlemens' Association, working together to sustain and improve the cattle industry in Florida.

## PIONEER COW HUNTERS

During a short twenty-year period when Florida was under British rule (1763–83), English planters and Creek Indians owned large herds of cattle in West Florida. Cowmen from Georgia and the Carolinas also spread into North Florida during that period. But it wasn't until Florida became a U.S. territory in 1821, when most of the remaining Spanish settlers departed for Cuba, that a new kind of settler appeared on the Florida frontier. As one news reporter wrote:

*They came with the Declaration of Independence in one hand and a carbine in the other…to a vast untamed wilderness stretching between Pensacola, and St. Augustine inhabited by wild animals and a few white settlers. Wolves, panthers and bear prowled the pine barrens, often attacking the livestock and settlers. Only Indian paths and a few remnants of the Spanish Trail linked the Indian villages and provided an overland route between the two towns. It seemed a dangerous, forbidding territory to many, but to the hardy frontier herdsman, it was beacon of hope, independence and freedom.*

Many homesteaders of Scotch-Irish descent began moving to Florida from Georgia and the Carolinas. Some who came were already experienced herders, and they hunted and trapped in addition to raising livestock. Some who came were successful planters with means and affluence, and they longed to improve their fortunes. But most were poor, bringing with them all their worldly goods—a few scrawny cows, an oven and frying pan, some pewter dishes, tools, a rifle, a cow whip and a wagon drawn by a horse or oxen.

Settlers preferred Florida to the West because of its closer proximity to the coast, milder climate and the fact its grazing land could support cattle all year long. Regardless of whether these early Florida pioneers were planters, herdsmen or yeoman farmers, according to Joe Akerman in his book *Florida*

Turn-of-the-century Florida cowboys. *Florida Archives.*

*Cowman: A History of Florida Cattle Raising*, they quickly found out that the pine lands, the broad river plains and the palmetto prairies were best for raising stock, and cattle raising remained the area's principal occupation until the late antebellum period.

The number of cattle in Florida increased dramatically between the 1840s and the Civil War. Though trade with Cuba was halted during the Civil war, early pioneer families, like the Roberts, Carltons, Lykes, Summerlins, McKays, Hendrys, Aldermans, Wells and many others, reestablished trade with Cuba after the war and brought back Florida's economy. Left with useless Confederate money after the war, they insisted on being paid in gold coin. At this time, Florida was America's leading exporter of cattle. This trade became the foundation of Florida's vast agricultural economy. Many of Florida's oldest and largest businesses began as cattle ranching operations during this time, and these operations depended, of course, on Spanish cattle and horses.

These early pioneers were sometimes referred to as *Crackers*, the term originating from various sources but most commonly known to refer to the loud crack of the cowman's whip used to move cattle. They often brought foundation herds that interbred with the wild Spanish scrub cattle. Early Crackers moved their cattle from place to place in search of better grazing land, often living out of covered wagons or a type of lean-to in order to create a cow camp until they could construct a simple cabin out of cypress and pine. Durable, sturdy and unpretentious like the Cracker himself, the cabin was built to withstand the ill winds of nature. Even after becoming wealthy, many Cracker families preferred living in these humble, durable dwellings, virtually unchanged by time.

An early Cracker cattle family were the Reuben Carltons, writes Joe Akerman in *The Florida Cowman*, who traveled east from Fort Myers around 1870 to graze their cattle on ranch land in present-day St. Lucie County. Reuben Carlton had nine children, and part of the family's group included a schoolteacher who lived and traveled with them. Her name was Miss Elder Andrews. The family settled near Ten Mile, named

Early Florida cattleman Jake Summerlin. *Florida Archives.*

The Carltons, one of the state's pioneer ranching families, have been influential in Florida since 1843. The family raises cattle and grows citrus in Hardee, Highlands, De Soto and Okeechobee Counties. Doyle Carlton served as governor from 1929 to 1933, and Doyle Carlton Jr. served three terms as state senator. Mildred and Doyle Carlton Jr. established the pioneer village at the Florida State Fair. *Florida Archives.*

for its location ten miles east of the Atlantic coast. Around the same time, the Paynes, Hendrys and Hoggs settled nearby and raised large herds of cattle. They had an unwritten agreement that if anyone found their neighbor's cattle mixed in with theirs, they would pen them up and return them to their owner. Families built their homes on their homestead sites, but the cattle roamed over a large, unfenced range owned by the state.

Though Florida cattlemen did not have to face blizzards like their western counterparts, they suffered through hurricanes and floods. "During the 1873 flood, all of the families near Fort Pierce had to seek safety on an old Indian mound about five miles southwest of Fort Pierce," recalled Mrs. Charlie Boykin, a daughter of Rueben Carlton, who said she also remembers seeing sharks swimming in a grove that now adjoins their home. In order to get back to their homes, most families had to swim their horses part of the way, following the road beds. When one hurricane came, the Carltons, fearing a tidal wave, ripped up the flooring from their ranch house and made a flat barge to carry the women and children to safety. Thankfully, no tidal wave came, but they used the barge to tow the family to safety at the old Indian mound, where they rode out the storm.

According to the Chaires interview from the *Osceola Sun*'s September 11, 1976 issue, "Most of what a Cracker family needed was grown, hunted, or learned from the Indians. Wild game was readily available, as were edible wild plants like, persimmon, guava, huckleberries and gooseberries as well as cassava plants....Once Cracker families learned to grow sugar cane, annual sugar cane grinding led to syrup and candy making."

# THE COW HUNT

Many Cracker cowmen used herding practices that had been passed down from the people of the marshy coastal regions of Andalusia, Spain, and the hill regions of Britain and Ireland. In Andalusia, ranchers living in towns hired cowhands (vaqueros), who marked or branded the cattle, managed them from horses and moved them to different locations during the year. In the fall, the animals were sold to drovers, who used dogs and whips to drive them to markets or slaughterhouses. The primary practice of the roundup, or what the Florida Cracker cowman referred to as a cow hunt, used long, braided cow whips made of deer hide to "pop" the cattle out of the dense Florida brush and scrub, and they frequently needed a good cow dog to flush them out. As it was in other cattle cultures, the roundup was one of the cowman's most important activities. Beginning in the early fall, late winter or early spring, it required long hours in the saddle in all types of unpredictable Florida weather.

Captain F.A. Hendry, who later became a Southwest Florida cattle king, described an 1870s cow hunt:

> *Cattle pens are erected at convenient points for gathering in the stock....Pens are built of pine logs generally, or sometimes of cabbage palms and cypress... located from 10 to 15 miles apart....The hunting parties generally consist of from six to ten active young men, well mounted on tough, hardy and fleet ponies. Each party has a wagon and team to transport the camp equipage and supplies, and each cowboy is equipped with a good cow whip, tin cup, wallet and saddlebags.*

Cow hunters were in the saddle by sunrise, and the woods were filled with the noise of bleating calves and bellowing cows, states Joe Akerman in *The Florida Cowman*. Each crew had a foreman, whose duties included giving orders to bring in cattle from a certain area, numbering the gathered cattle and keeping track of the number of calves marked. By nightfall, all the cattle of that day's hunt were either penned or collected on burns, where there was plenty of green wire grass.

The burn resulted from the annual burning that was necessary to create a pine-wire grass forage complex for grazing. This technique was practiced by both the Indians and the Spanish in order to ensure fresh, tender grass grew for the game and livestock. Normally, early Florida Cracker cattlemen burned at least one-third of the range each year for grazing, according to Florida Cattlemen's Association notes Mealor and Prunty.

Eventually, a large herd, numbering from five hundred to one thousand head, would be collected and driven to a certain point for sale or continued holding, as documented by newspaper writer Myrtle Hilliard Crow in her article "Cattle Raising in Early Florida." The cow hunters, often traveling a mile or more apart, communicated with each other across the range by popping their cow whips and giving the cattleman's cow whoop. Captain Hendry said that as the herd approached a given point, to the inexperienced ear, it sounded like an approaching tornado. When the cattle were eventually driven into large holding pens, the weary, hungry cow hunters would retire to camp, where they would often feast on venison steak, rice or hominy, biscuits and gallons of strong coffee. They ate from tin plates and cups and used iron spoons and pocketknives. Their day's work completed, the boys filled their pipes and gathered around a cheerful pine knot fire to smoke while they recounted the incidents of the day. After these yarns were spun, the blankets would be spread on the ground, and all would find rest.

Marking and branding was the hardest physical work of the roundup. After the beef cattle were selected and separated, the rest were turned back to the open range. Sometimes, Cracker cowmen were paid by the number of cattle they marked and branded. Cattleman John T. Lesley's diary shows that in 1880, he paid $82 to a cowman for marking 164 calves. Three years later, he recorded that he paid a cowman $876 for branding 702 cattle, driving 285 cattle and selling 205 steers and cows for him.

The work of cow hunting and branding might continue for months, and in some cases, two hunts would take place in one year. On some occasions, families with cattle interests banded together during the cow hunts and marking. In Levy County, for instance, the Clyatt, Hayes, Heir and Hardee families would join up for their annual cow hunt. "Some cow hunts were even like a family reunion," recalled Mrs. Walter Bishop, formerly of Osceola County, Florida. "Relatives from all over would pitch in and help in some way, whether it was cooking food for the drovers or hunting cattle in the bayheads. The girls would also help in the penning and roundup."

In some cases, boats had to be used to get all the stock together. Jargo Clark of Madison, Florida, recalled hunting cattle along the Appalachicola during spring floods: "The cattle would climb up on the ridges trying to escape the water but would stay there until someone got them out. We would have to use boats to get in there....Once we got them off the islands, we would wade along beside them, urging them on. Sometimes I would get over my head and have to grab them on the tail of a cow until she pulled me to shallow water."

## THE CATTLE DRIVE

While cattle were driven relatively short distances during the cow hunts, extended drives, sometimes covering hundreds of miles, had to be made to herd cattle to markets, railheads and ports. Such cattle drives from Florida had long preceded the more well known cattle drives originating in Texas that took place along the Chisholm, Goodnight and Shawnee Trails.

Some of the longest cattle drives out of Florida took place during the Civil War, when the Confederate army was receiving three-fourths of its beef from Florida. These drives, which might have easily been over three hundred miles long, often originated near or at Fort Meade, and the cattle were generally driven by Confederate cowboy soldiers, or what was known as the Cow Cavalry. Aside from dealing with the regular hazards of driving wild cattle, the Cow Cavalry was also faced with the danger of Union patrols and Confederate deserters trying to steal stock. It was estimated that Yankee patrols stole over 4,500 head of beef in 1863 in the Fort Myers area.

One member of the cattle guard related to the late Theodore Lesley the following incident that occurred on a cattle drive from Fort Meade to Savannah, Georgia: "When they forded the Altamaha River northwest of Brunswick, Georgia, several hundred civilians gathered to watch. While crossing, two cattle out of the herd were drowned, and once pulled ashore, several of the drovers butchered them. They took most of the meat, but when the crowd was told they could have what was left…within one hour not one horn, hoof or tail was left. It shows you how hungry folks were then."

One of the most popular trails over which cattle were driven to Punta Rassa in the 1880s was sometimes called the Sam Summerlin Trail. Usually originating at St. Augustine from the pens of Venancio Sanchez, the trail crossed the state to Braddock's Pens in Volusia County. From there, the cattle were moved down to Holden's Prairies on the St. Johns River and then to Hart's Pens north of Orlando. Summerlin's drovers would buy more and more beeves as they moved on, and they usually found the largest concentration of cattle at Dave Mizell's pens, near Lake Conway. From Mizell's pens, the cattle were usually herded down the Old Fort Brooke–Fort Mellon Military Road. Crossing at Shingle Creek, the restless cattle would be trailed along the General Jessup Trail, across Bennett Creek and onto the Secret Indian Trail to a point south of Lake Tohopekaliga, where they were then taken to Shiver's cow pens at Canoe Creek. From there, the large

A turn-of-the-century cowboy with a Cracker horse at an open range roundup near Fort McCoy. *Florida Archives.*

herds would be driven to Captain Ab Johnson's large pens near Whittier. Eventually, the drovers would make contact with cattle traders at Fort Drum, moving there to Fort Bassinger, where the herd was usually completed. Most of the ranchers south of Bassinger drove their own cattle to ports on the East and West Florida coasts.

## Shipping Ports

One of the best ports on the Gulf Coast of Florida was Punta Rassa. In an article in the *Fort Myers Press* from November 29, 1884, Punta Rassa was described as being of "sufficient depth of water for vessels of adequate size." The article continues:

> *There was good holding ground for anchors and a safe harbor. The official coast chart shows twenty-four feet of water at the wharf.... The distance from Punta Rassa to Key West is one hundred and twenty miles and from Key West to Havana about ninety, making two hundred and ten miles in*

*all. A steamship can easily make the run from Punta Rassa to Havana, touching at Key West, in twenty-four hours. All steamships on their way to Cuba had to stop in Key West to clear customs.*

Civil War captain Francis Asbury Hendry (1833–1917) was one of the originators of the Cuban cattle trade from Punta Rassa via Key West. He owned large tracts of land in the Fort Thompson area, and it was reported that at one time, he owned as many as fifty thousand head of cattle. At his Fort Thompson ranch, close to the shipping port of Punta Rassa, he fenced in twenty-five thousand acres and began planting guinea grass and other varieties of grass in his pastures. He also introduced pure-blood Jerseys, crossing them with scrub cattle, which developed a hardy, valuable strain of cattle that was hard to surpass.

Captain Hendry constructed his own pens and log wharves that extended several hundred yards into the gulf at Punta Rassa, states author Sara Nell Gran in *Florida Cattle Frontier: Over Four Hundred Years of Cattle Raising*. He operated the wharves not only for his own use but also for the convenience of other cattle shippers. In 1878, he sold these facilities to Jake Summerlin for $10,000. In the beginning, workmen used block and tackle to load the cattle onto the steamships, which carried six hundred head at a time to Cuba. Later, the docks were built so that cranes would not have to be used to load the cattle. The cattle were corralled in a large pen, which was connected by a chute or a boarded driveway to the vessel, and bunches of a dozen head were driven on board.

After giving up his medical practice to raise and export cattle in present-day Citrus, Hernando, Pasco, Hillsborough and Pinelles Counties, Dr. Howell Tyson Lykes partnered with Captain W.H. Towles of Perry and Fort Myers to export cattle to Cuba. Their first two schooners were the 108-foot-long motor schooner *Dr. Lykes* and the little steamer *Fanita*. Dr. Lykes married Almeria Belle McKay, the daughter of Captain James McKay, and had eight children, one girl and seven boys. The boys worked during their vacations as deckhands and cowboys, and eventually, they all went into either the shipping or cattle business. The two oldest sons, Fred and H.T., were sent to Havana to open a family office at the end of the Spanish-American War, consolidating Cuban ranches and opening Cuba's first meatpacking plant. Their ships imported cattle from Florida, Texas, Central America and South America, and four years after Dr. Lykes died, the firm Lykes Brothers was incorporated in Florida. By 1922, Lykes Bros. Steamship Company had become America's largest shipping line and the largest producer of cattle and meatpacker in

*Left*: A steamship at Punta Rassa, a wharf where cattle were hurriedly pushed along chutes and crowded into every available spot on board the schooners that plowed the waters between Punta Rassa, Tampa, St. Andrews Bay, Charlotte Harbor and Cuba. Many ships carried two hundred or more head of cattle per trip. *Florida Archives.*

*Right*: Early Florida cattlemen. *Florida Archives.*

Florida. Today, the Lykes ranch in South Florida covers 337,000 acres and ranks as one of the top-three cattle producers in the United States.

## Stampedes and Other Hazards

Although there was no fear of Indian attacks or Union patrols in the 1870s, the business of herding and driving cattle still had many hazards. One of the constant fears when working these wild cattle was the probability of a stampede. As a cowman, A.B. Wright of De Soto County said, "It didn't take much to get a bunch of cows jumping. A bear, a clap of thunder, or even the crack of a stick might cause 'em to break loose. And it usually happened on the darkest night. Still, I've been run over, and stomped but never had a bone broken."

African American rancher Lawrence Silas of Osceola County said that he always worried about his anchored horses when cattle broke loose: "I've have seen them stomped out as flat as a piece of paper." He also remembered a stampede at Fort Bassinger one night that involved about 1,100 cattle that all seemed to jump at once. "The cowboys heard them in time and scattered like quail, and no one was hurt, but we didn't find them until the next morning, and most were bogged down in a large swamp. We knowed the ground was too soft for 'em to get across. You couldn't see no cows at all. Wasn't a thing we could do. All you could see was horns, just a whole lake of horns," Silas recalled.

When tethered, corralled or bunched, Cracker ponies were also known to stampede on occasion. Cattleman E.L. Lesley recalled an incident that occurred at a cow camp near Kissimmee in the late 1800s:

> *An old timer had been hunting rattlesnakes to sell to a zoo up North, and had stopped in late at night to share the campfire. He was naturally welcomed, and he hitched his wagon near where the horses fed up. No one knew there were snakes in the wagon but the old man, as the bed was covered in timbers. About four o'clock the next morning the horses were let loose to come up and feed. One of the horses backed up against the wagon and started rubbing himself against the side. Suddenly those rattlers began buzzing like a bunch of hornets. It was a sound every cowman and every horse on the Florida range knew. Chaos reigned for a few minutes as the horses ran for the woods, and the cowmen jumped out of their bedrolls. One cow man was so excited that he carried his bedroll out in the woods as he ran—and never found it!*

Other dangers existed on these drives, or cow hunts. E.L. Lesley remembered how alligators attacked two of his best cow dogs. Once, when he was driving cattle across the river near Fort Kissimmee, several alligators took off after his dogs: "We shot those gators with our pistols, but they came on. We even hit the gators with our whips, but they seemed to be dog hungry….We had to hold the dogs in our arms in order to save them."

When visiting Florida in 1895, well-known artist Frederic Remington noted that Florida bulls and steers often turned on cowboys: "It frequently happens that when the herd is being driven quietly along, a wild bull will turn on the drovers, charging at once. The bulls often become so maddened in their forays that they would drop and die in their tracks, for which strange fact no one can account." The explanation was no doubt found in Remington's imagination.

Cracker pioneer cattle king Captain Francis Asbury Hendry owned thirty thousand acres in Hendry County (later named for him), and he recounted the story of an old vicious "cradled headed" bull named Old Frostysides: "[As] I was a turnin' the point of the bayhead, Old Frosty come out of the swamp like a tornado, with a great load of vines around his horns. I spurred Jack and squared myself before him. Then I give him a few right smart cracks with my drag, tryin' to turn him into the herd, but he kept comin' for me full tilt. Back of me was a point of sawgrass, and there wan't no way to run 'cept into the bog." After getting thrown from his mount into the bog,

Hendry remembered, "the first thing I seen when I raised up out of the mud was Old Frosty's eyes lookin' green at me, his tongue out, with ropes of slobber streamin' from his mouth and nostrils. He was all set to run me through.…How I did it, I don't know, but I snatched my hat off and swung at him. The point of one horn stuck right through the crown and rested square over Old Frosty's eyes so he couldn't see a thing. I guess it's still there yet, and I hope it'll rot there."

## Women and Children

Public education on the Florida frontier was almost nonexistent in the nineteenth century, remembered cattleman Robert Griffin in an interview conducted by Joe Ackerman on December 22, 1975. When Jane Elizabeth Parker, the wife of cattle king John Parker, attended school in an old log schoolhouse, the curriculum was limited to *Webster's Elementary* and *Parley's History*. The Bible, she said, was her true guidebook, from which she taught her children to read and provided them with a sound spiritual foundation. Jane Elizabeth Parker's obituary from 1891 reflects the hardships and contributions of a heroic pioneer: "Her long and useful life was connected with the history of our early frontier.…Few, under such circumstances of extreme poverty, privation and painful disease, trials and sufferings…would have survived the ordeal, especially when there was no promise of relief, respite or change."

Sometimes, cattlemen gave each of their newborn children a calf and a new brand and continued the practice with each subsequent birthday. "When the child was old enough to start working cows, he had the nucleus of a herd. This practice also helped keep the family together," described cattleman Robert Griffin, Fort Pierce, Florida, December 22, 1975, in an interview with Joe Ackerman.

Though women sometimes went on cow hunts and cattle drives, these were generally thought to be the jobs of men. Women were mostly in charge of keeping the pioneer home running smoothly—educating the children, protecting the children and stock from predators, handling stock sales—while men were hunting or on cattle drives. It was a dangerous time, according to news reporter Myrtle Hilliard Crow, "when women were capable and fearless—it really took a special kind of fortitude to withstand the hardships and make real helpmates.…They were capable of using their guns efficiently and went armed whenever necessary. They endured the screams of the wildcats and panthers…and the paralyzing war whoop, which was a scream and a yell.…That war whoop, once heard, was never forgotten." As another woman put it, "There is nothing a woman left alone on a ranch can't imagine."

## FROM COWBOY TO CATTLEMAN

While working cattle for someone else, Crackers were able to evolve from cowhand to rancher because of the availability of the vast, open grazing lands and the large number of unbranded cattle that roamed the woodlands and prairies. Lawrence Silas, the son of a formerly enslaved man, told the tale of how he transformed from a cowboy to a cattleman: "I went into the cattle business just like my father did. Bought a cow or two at a time, sold my *hes* and put the money into *shes*. Sarah, my wife, took in sewing and kept the house going.…I put all that I could rake and scrape into the herd.…We came to have quite a few."

Jacob Summerlin (1820–1893) was reportedly the first child born in the Florida Territory. He was said to have started working cattle and cracking cow whips by the age of seven. At sixteen, he settled in Central Florida, where he owned vast herds in what are now Orange and Osceola Counties. By 1858, he and his brothers, Samuel and Clarence, were selling cattle to Spanish buyers from Cuba. As the Summerlins drove cattle across the state to Tampa, they sent riders ahead to inform cattle owners they were approaching, and cattlemen who wanted to sell would pen their stock as the Summerlins approached. By the time they reached the west coast of Florida, they had amassed thousands of head of cattle. Charging between three and eight dollars a head, Jake and his boys would receive between ten and twelve dollars in Spanish gold doubloons.

Jacob Summerlin became one of the richest men in Florida before he reached the age of forty. He bought parcels of land in Southwest Florida, as well as a warf at Punta Rassa. After the Civil War, he donated land to establish a school in Bartow, opened the Summerlin Hotel in Orlando and donated land for Lake Eola Park. He also became Orlando City Council's first president.

## LEGENDS

As featured in "The Life and Times of Bone Mizell" by Jim Bob Tinsley, the most talked about and colorful of the early Florida cow hunters was

Morgan Boneparte Mizell, also known as "Bone," who was born in a time of frequent frontier violence. The American West in the late 1880s was a place of lawlessness, and the open ranges of cow country in Florida at that time were no different. In DeSoto County and the surrounding area, there were cattle wars, family feuds, rustles, assassinations, vigilante hunts, hangings, lynchings, cowtown duels and fence cuttings. It was said that "Kentucky had her Daniel Boone, Tennessee had her Davy Crockett, but Florida had her champion, 'Bone Mizell,' the pioneer cowboy humorist."

Legendary Cracker cowhunter Bone Mizell. *Florida Archives.*

Bone Mizell was a celebrity in Florida's cow country—a hard-drinking, fun-loving cow hunter who was the center of attention wherever he went. He was even the subject of a painting by Frederic Remington in 1895. He made the front page of a metropolitan New York newspaper, and a ballad was written about one of his exploits. He worked with cows practically all his life, first for his father, periodically for cattle barons and occasionally for himself. Held in high esteem by his cow hunter peers, he was said to "outrope, outride, outshoot and outdrink" any cowman in Florida. He never married, never owned a home and seldom slept in a bed.

Every year during the spring roundup, cattleman Ziba King rewarded the cowhand who put the King brand on the largest number of calves by giving him a few head of cattle for himself. In 1892, Bone acquired one of King's cows in an irregular fashion that earned him the reputation of being able to earmark cattle without a knife, should the need arise. A cowboy who witnessed the incident described the curious event:

> *One day I was riding the range with Buck King, the boss, and Bone. A thin old cow was discovered at the edge of a thicket of thornbush. She was a pugnacious old beast, evidently planning Bones' discomfiture. Buck challenged: "Rope her and put your mark on her, and you can have her." Bone accepted the challenge and soon had a rope on the cow's horns. He dismounted quickly with knife in hand, but the old cow was hard to handle. She dragged Bone into the thicket, where he lost his knife and had most of his clothes ripped off by the thorny scrub. He finally emerged a sorry spectacle, dragging his lariat. King chided him on being bested by an old range cow.*

*"But I put my mark on her," declared Bone.*
*"How could you mark her? I saw you lose your knife," answered King.*
*"Marked her with my teeth—just as good as I could have done it with a knife." declared Bone.*
*We ran the old cow out of the brush and verified Bone's statement—he had put his mark in her ears with his teeth.*

Bone's skill as a cowboy was legendary. One day, he and some of the Kings were driving a herd of wild cattle back to the ranch headquarters when a young bull broke away and disappeared into the thicket. The cowboys searched for the animal but finally gave up and moved on with the rest of the herd. Only Bone stayed behind, still looking for the bull.

Around three o'clock the next morning, Bone rode in with the lost bull and, with enough yelling, whistling and bellowing, woke the rest of the crew. When asked how he found his way back in the pitch dark, Bone implied that he and the bull had navigated their way together: "Well, I'd drive him for a while, and then he'd drive me for a while."

In the fall of 1896, Bone helped a friend out of an illegal skirmish similar to one he had experienced before. The friend was arrested for butchering a cow of questionable ownership. Although he was well known in De Soto County as an upstanding citizen, Bone was worried about his upcoming trial. Bone made him an offer: "You buy me a John B. Stetson hat, and I'll get you out of this in two minutes."

"How?" asked the friend.

"Just have them call me as a witness," Bone answered.

The cowboy agreed.

At the trial, various witnesses were questioned about the earmarks, brands, time of day and other facts concerning the case. Bone was put on the stand and testified that he had seen the alleged butchering. When asked where he was at the time, he replied, "Bee Branch."

"Where's Bee Branch?" queried the prosecutor.

"Everybody knows where Bee Branch is," answered Bone. "It's two or three hundred yards over in the next county."

The defense called for a dismissal on the grounds that the defendant could not be tried in Arcadia for an offense committed in an adjoining county. The case was thrown out of court, and Bone got his new Stetson.

One day, a judge fined Bone twenty dollars for wearing a hat into his courtroom. Bone calmly counted out twenty dollars and then an additional twenty and placed the money on the judge's bench. "You better take forty, suh, 'cause I walked in heah with my hat on, and I'm gonna walk out the same way."

Another time, Bone attended a camp revival meeting after a night out on the town. Hungover, hot and thirsty, Bone set his sights on the big pitcher of water on the pulpit. Bone was the first to volunteer when the preacher called for sinners to be prayed for at the alter. While the preacher and congregation closed their eyes in prayer, Bone turned the pitcher up and gulped down all the water.

His picturesque life was memorialized in the following song by Ruby Leach Carson:

*"The Ball of Bone Mizell"*

*Oh, come all you rounders, and I will tell*
*About the Florida Cowboy named Bone Mizell.*
*He stood six feet, three, from his hat to the ground,*
*And he looked just like a scarecrow come riding into town.*

*He could rope a cow and brand him before you could say his name.*
*Cattle driving, bullwhip cracking was his claim to fame.*
*He was born in Central Florida about 1863.*
*He rode off in the sunset and into history.*

*Yeah, he was king of the old Cracker cowboys,*
*Riding forever across the old scrub trails.*
*Sing us a song and a story to tell*
*About the legend of Bone Mizell.*

*Some say he was born with a bullwhip in his hand,*
*And his first words to his daddy were, "A Cracker I am."*
*At six, he dove into the water and drove a herd of manatee,*
*And at ten, he roped a hurricane and rode it out to sea.*

*Yeah, Bone Mizell was born with Florida in his soul,*
*And in 1921 the moonshine finally took its toll.*
*He's gone but not forgotten. If you listen carefully,*
*You can still hear old Bone laughing in the breeze.*

## MODERN DAY FLORIDA CATTLEMEN AND CATTLEWOMEN

As Florida moved into the twentieth century, so did the roots of the cattle industry, carried on by the men and women who embodied that heritage, steeped in a deep love and reverence for the land and love for the horses they rode and the cattle they raised. The following portraits are but a sampling of the men, women and their families who live this culture today.

### *Bud Adams*

Alto Lee "Bud" Adams was born on April 4, 1926, Easter Sunday, in Fort Pierce, Florida. Bud's father, Alto Adams Sr., was a Fort Pierce attorney who gained recognition representing family members who were gunned down by the infamous Ashley Gang. Alto Sr. bought some horses and joined forces with another local lawyer, Thad Carlton, and invested in a herd of cattle. Thad was a member of the multigenerational Carlton family, whose roots in Florida go back to the early 1800s. At that time, western St. Lucie County, like most of Florida, was all open range. That meant you didn't have to own the land to use it for grazing cattle. Fencing wasn't required by law until 1949, so every cattleman and his cows were free to roam at will—just like the Seminoles, who still lived in chickees in the area, grazed their own free-roaming Cracker cattle.

Although Bud lived in town growing up, before he was a teenager, he was making cattle drives to the middle of the state. His father had purchased thousands of acres of open range for next to nothing from a man whose taxes were in arrears. He witnessed steers charging over the banks of the Kissimmee River, where they were received by cowhands working for Lykes brothers on the other side. When Bud was thirteen, his father was nominated to serve on Florida's Supreme Court, so the family moved to Tallahassee. Bud remained there for the rest of his childhood, but he still rode the range in the summers with legendary Irlo Bronson, whom he referred to as "Florida's greatest cattleman." Bud went on cattle hunts and cattle drives and slept on the ground around a campfire with all the cowboys. "Irlo Bronson taught me most of what I know about the illustrious heritage of ranching and its down-home egalitarian ways," said Bud.

During World War II, Bud went to Emory University to study nuclear physics, but the war ended before he could get his commission. "But you know, we use some of what I learned every day. We are governed by the laws of

Bud Adams with his sister Elaine, Great Florida Cattle Drive '95. *Jon Kral, Adams Ranch.*

physics, whether it's the way the water will run, how the heat will be dispersed or the air and everything else." After the war, Bud continued his education at the University of Florida, where he majored in economics. Though he had many opportunities to go into law and politics, he simply said, "Politics was never my cup of tea....I'd like to go home and run the ranch."

At that time, St. Lucie County was only one-fifteenth of the size it is today, and it had gone almost unchanged since the 1800s, when the first white pioneer settlers arrived. "When I got here in 1948," Bud said, "Orange Avenue wasn't extended out west like it is today. It was still a grade, and a group of Indians lived a couple miles away. I had no source of help and was running the ranch myself. So, I would get the Seminoles—Sam Jones and his boys—to help me herd the cattle. They'd bring their Cracker horses to the ranch. They were expert cowboys."

When Bud married Dorothy "Dot" Snively, a former Cypress Gardens belle from Winter Haven (and the best-looking woman at FSU, he added), she agreed to move to the ranch, and they lived in the cypress house he built for her for the rest of their lives. Dot shared her husband's pioneering spirit. They had three sons, Lee, Robbie and Mike, who all grew up sharing Bud's interest in cattle and agriculture and love of the land.

Although he never studied genetics in college, Bud was gifted with a quick mind and grasped the intricacies of genetics in agriculture and its markets. He realized that Florida cattlemen needed to up their game if they were to stay in business. Even though Spanish cattle had adapted well in Florida, they were small and did not meet the standards of the prosperous postwar consumer. He read every book he could find on genetics and realized that he would need to create a new breed of cattle altogether, one that would produce better meat but could also withstand the sweltering conditions of a semitropical environment. He made thousands of crossbreeds between Brahman and Hereford cattle that gradually evolved to meet the conditions he'd hoped for. "The ones that worked, I bred. The others, I culled. Gradually, the cream rose to the top," he wrote in his booklet *The Old Florida*. "They were heat-tolerant, heavy weaning and pretty good beef-type cattle."

In 1969, the USDA realized that he had, in fact, created a better kind of cow: the Braford. That same year, Bud chartered the International Braford Breeders, now known as the United Braford Breeders, to control the quality of the breed. He was also a pioneering advocate for conserving and protecting the land for future generations. "A perfect world is one with good balance of man, animals and the land. Our planning and preparation is not in years, it is in generations." said Bud. "The Adams Ranch conservation program lies at the heart of our business. The pastures are never overgrazed, so the roots run deep. That helps the topsoil retain its fertility, so the grass grows thick and beautiful. The hammocks of Adams Ranch are the longest tract of hammocks left in the Indian River District. We hope to see it preserved....At my age, I am concerned about how the land will look fifty to one hundred years from now." His ranch has won almost every award a ranch can win, including the 1997 National Cattlemen's Beef Association's Cattle Business of the Century Award and the Florida Fish and Wildlife Commission's 2013 Landowner of the Year Award.

Mike took over as president when Bud retired. The running of the Madison County ranch location was assumed by Lee, and the ranch's citrus groves are managed by Robbie. LeeAnn Adams, one of Bud's granddaughters, coordinates public policy and all the details related to different government regulations and programs, and the Adams legacy continues on.

Bud worked alongside many of the founding families of modern-day Florida. He was a proud member of the Florida Cattlemen's Association, serving as president in 1958. He always had a firm handshake, and his word was his bond. His love for the Florida prairies and woodlands was evident not only in his holistic approach to land management but also in his photographs of the natural beauty of the animals, people and land. Bud passed away peacefully on September 22, 2017, surrounded by his family.

*Portions of Mr. Bud's biography were taken from the* Indian River *magazine 2015 edition, with permission from the Adams family.*

## *Jim Alderman*

James Elliot Alderman was born in Fort Pierce, Florida, on November 1, 1936, and passed away on June 10, 2021. He grew up in Fort Pierce and spent most of his free time working cattle on the ranch while going to school. As a young cowboy, Alderman learned the essential jobs that came with being a cattle rancher, participating in all phases of the operation. After Alderman graduated from Fort Pierce High School, he attended the University of Florida for four years. In his sophomore year, he made the decision to major in prelaw and go to law school.

*It was a tough decision, but my father and grandfather were running the ranch at that time, and there wasn't room for another partner. I went to law school for three years, and during that time, I met my future wife, Jennie Thompson, on a blind date. She was working as a medical research technologist at the University of Florida Medical School. A mutual friend from Fort Pierce, who worked in the same lab, arranged the date. We dated a couple years, and we were married in 1961, before I graduated with a law degree. After I graduated, we returned to St. Lucie County, and I practiced law as a general practitioner attorney, helping whomever came through the door. Two years later, September 1, 1963, our only child, James A. "Jimmy" Alderman, was born.*

As a sixth-generation Floridian from a heritage family with 180 years in ranching and farming, he was president of the Florida Cattlemen's Association. And as a lawyer, he became a judge, culminating his law career with an appointment by former Governor Rueben Askew as a justice on the Florida Supreme Court (1978–85), where he also served as chief justice (1982–84). He was also the sixty-seventh justice of the court. Alderman holds the distinction of being the only judge to serve on all four levels of the Florida courts.

His family has deep roots in the Florida cattle industry. In the 1830s, James Alderman, Jim's great-great-grandfather, was the first of his family to migrate from Georgia to North Florida, where he and his family remained until the end of the Second Seminole War (1835–1842). After a few years, the Aldermans left North Florida and settled in what is now Manatee County. "James Alderman's son, William, is my great-grandfather, born in 1828. After the Civil War, he and his family moved to the lower Kissimmee River Valley at Micco Bluff, north of Basinger, where he died in 1893," said Alderman.

*My grandfather B.E. Alderman Sr., "Teet," moved with his family, in 1908, from Bassinger to Fort Pierce. In the late 1930s, he purchased several thousand acres twenty miles west of fort Pierce on the St. Lucie–Okeechobee County line. He moved his herd of Cracker cattle from the open range to his newly purchased land.…When my grandfather first bought the property, Seminole Indians lived on the land and remained there until the last family member moved in the 1960s. Sam Jones was the patriarch of the family. He had several children who all worked on the ranch during roundups. They lived in traditional Seminole houses called chickees, with an elevated platform for the preparation of food and slept under a thatched palmetto roof. Another group of Seminoles lived a short distance away at Cow Creek.*

*When roundup time came, cowboys spent the night on the range in a cow camp under a small shelter with a table to eat on. The camp cooked biscuits, beans, rice, and on the first day of camping, they killed a yearling for beef. The cowboys slept on a platform with a mosquito net over their bedrolls. Commuting to and from the ranch was not an option for us cowboys. It wasn't until the 1940s that Orange Avenue, the road from Fort Pierce, was paved past the ranch.*

In 1995, at the height of his judicial career, Alderman's loyalty was divided. Although he loved the law, he was conflicted when his father, B.E. Alderman Jr., became ill and there was no one to manage the family ranch. Alderman, then chief justice of the Florida Supreme Court, had to choose between law and ranching. His loyalty to his family tipped the scale, and he chose to resign as chief justice. He and his family returned home to fulfill another vital role in Alderman's life: "I always worked on the ranch during vacations and weekends from Tallahassee and planned to come back home, but not this soon."

"When I returned home, my sister Joyce DeLoney and I and our families formed a partnership, which is known as Alderman DeLoney Ranch. Our brand is 'OK' joined," said Alderman. As Alderman reestablished his life as a full-time cattle rancher, he and his wife, Jennie, built their two-story wooden home on the ranch in Okeechobee County. Jennie raised sheep and learned to shear and weave their wool into yarn. She volunteered her time and talent to schoolchildren, teaching them about this disappearing art. She was always involved in many aspects of the ranch. Jennie Alderman passed away on March 17, 2010.

Jim Alderman's son, Jimmy, eventually joined him as the assistant ranch manager, leaving his job designing and testing weapons for America's special forces. He said, "I hunted a lot on the ranch and have a long-time interest in firearms; however, I'm the only one here to continue the family heritage. I plan to hold onto and preserve the ranch. My son also has an interest in the ranch and following in the footsteps of his grandfather's legal career."

With an increase in the number of large corporate ranches throughout Florida, Alderman Sr. maintained a medium-size family ranch that he hoped to pass on to his and his sister's heirs. Due to the large assessment of federal "inheritance taxes," Alderman stressed that "a rancher has to plan for retirement with a good estate planning attorney to preserve the land." In many instances, the heirs of small family ranches have difficulty paying the inheritance taxes and, as a result, sell the land. "Each situation is different," he explained. "Development in Florida is not going away, so seeing an estate planner to preserve the land for the next generation is important."

Today, the United States is confronted with complex global issues of economics, food shortages, increased crime and wars. However, Alderman Sr. maintained a positive outlook on the future, with faith in the law and the citizens of the United States. He believed "each generation looks at the present and thinks it's the worst of times and all is going downhill—then, looking back, it becomes the 'golden age.' Presently, we are not at war, but we are involved in a war where different rules apply to different people. This, too, shall pass. I am an optimist. I believe things are going to get better. I believe our country will survive, and we are going to come out of this financial bump in the road."

Even though there is creeping urbanization from coast to coast across the United States, Alderman Sr. said, "I believe the cattle industry is here to stay….United States beef is still the best in the world. But ranchers must do their part to encourage the next generation to appreciate the land and cattle. It is important to teach our children to love the land, care for cattle and pass on the heritage. It is a way of life."

*Judge Alderman's biograpy from* The Legacy of the Florida Pioneer Cow Hunters *by Nancy Dale was shared with permission from the author.*

## Ben Hill Griffin III

One of the oldest and most successful Florida heritage families is that of Ben Hill Griffin III. Though he heads a major diversified agricultural industry in Florida, he is not the image of a typical Wall Street executive. Instead, he is a gracious southern gentleman and cattle rancher whose family became some of Florida's oldest and largest citrus growers. He attributes the long-time success of the business to the philosophy and practice inspired by his grandfather and father: perseverance. He believes "perseverance is the main success formula to deal with hurricanes, freezes, droughts, insect infestations and catastrophic events faced by anyone who is in the agricultural industry." He said success is also achieved by "natural instinct and learned knowledge. This knowledge is the product of hard work, dedication and perseverance."

Griffin the III, raised in the citrus and cattle industries, worked his way to the top. "I helped my father work cattle and plant citrus. I learned as a young boy about perseverance, helping out on the farm through unpredictable natural disasters, and life was not easy. We had to 'make do.'" As words to live by, Griffin III recalled one of his father's greetings to guests at the ranch. He said, "If you want something, ask for it; if we don't have it, we will get it; and if we can't get it, we we'll show you how we can get along without it."

Ben Hill Griffin Jr. served eleven years in the Florida legislature and eight years in the Florida Senate. As a major contributor to his alma mater, the University of Florida, he provided scholarships and endowments. In 1989, the university named the home stadium of the Florida Gators (also known as the Swamp) in honor of Ben Hill Griffin Jr. "He wanted it to represent Ben Hill Griffin Jr., Ben Hill III and Ben Hill Griffin IV. Today, it is best known as Ben Hill Griffin Stadium," explained Griffin III.

Born on March 3, 1942, in Lake Wales, Griffin III is a traditional cattle rancher, as his father and grandfather were before him. "My grandfather migrated from Georgia after the Civil War to work in the phosphate mines in Fort Meade, eventually headin' up the operation. He had nothing more than a few dollars and meager belongings, but he had perseverance." Griffin Sr. moved the family to Frostproof when Griffin Jr. was just six years old. They cleared the land by gripping hoes, and they hauled water up from Lake Wales in buckets for the land and their personal needs."

The Griffin family has deep roots in Florida's history and has not lost touch with their heritage. Ben Hill Griffin III dedicates his life to preserving family traditions, especially the lifestyle of the pioneer cow hunter.

*As a cattle rancher, one of my practices is "marking and branding" to protect our herds, including pigs. We hire local cowboys to bring in young calves and do the jobs we can't do. Cattle can't read, so by marking and branding every year, we can monitor cattle rustling. Even after Governor Fuller Warren supported the passage of fence laws in the 1950s, cattle rustlers still operated* in Florida. *Today, cattle rustlers move into absentee owners' property, take twenty head and trailer them off to the stockyard. They also alter brands, or what we call "running brands," that you can easily see. Our cattle brand is "H," and all of our brands are registered in Tallahassee.*

In the days of Old Florida, cow hunters gained a learned knowledge of cattle by studying their habits. This could not be learned by reading a book; instead, it was learned while spending many long days and nights driving thousands of head over the long Florida Cracker trails to market. Griffin III still practices this tradition to acquire more "learned knowledge" about cattle, as evidenced from the following observations: "Cattle drift when it rains, but prior to a rain, they lie down and rest. When they get up, they have their tail and back into the wind," he explained.

*Cattle follow each other on a path. My father told my sister and me that they are "playing path." Cattle are also very territorial. If you have cows in fourteen pastures and each pasture is about 100 acres and you open all the gates and mix them up, they will go back to the pasture they were originally in. It is an instinct they have. Let's say you have twenty calves, I have seen one "baby sitter" cow lay down or stand with the calves while all the others are feeding in the pasture until their mothers return from grazing.*

*A lot of what I learned comes from common sense. For example, when you swim a horse across a river, if you aren't careful, you can push the horse's head down, and he will drown. You first have to get the horse swimming, so you can slip off the saddle and hold onto the saddle horn and swim alongside the horse. Once you get to more shallow water and the horses feet touch bottom, you can get back on. You must remember that your body makes up a lot of the horse's weight, and if the horse starts taking in water, it may drown. If you get in trouble, turn loose of the saddle horn and hold on to the horse's tail till you get to shallow water.*

When traveling many days along the trail, cowboys' knowledge of the woods provided them with food and sustenance. "They utilized the native cabbage palm, the state tree, for many uses," Griffin III explained.

*You can cut down the trunk and build a lean-to or log house. Like the Seminole Indians, you can weave the fronds together and make a shelter or roof. You can take the buds off the top of palm trees, split them up or unwrap the buds like an onion, until you reach the white core. Then you can score it, cut it*

Swamp cabbage. *Florida Archives.*

*into pieces and make swamp cabbage. My recipe for swamp cabbage was passed down through the family. I cook it with sugar, milk, water and bacon or horseradish for flavoring. By doing all of these things, you live it, and you learn to love it.*

*I love ranching, I rode my first Cracker horse when I was seven or eight years old. I had to stand on a stump to saddle and mount the horse. To get off, I also had to have a stump. Although we gathered up the cattle in the swamp, we never concerned ourselves with alligators, unless they would catch the cow dogs. I never had any snake bites either all the time we would go bird hunting in the fifties and sixties in the thick palmettos. We had a bird dog bitten by a rattlesnake once, but luckily, he lived. Only once did I see a Florida panther.*

"One of the worse epidemics to almost totally devastate the cattle industry occurred when I was a young boy," recalled Griffin III. "I lived in the cattle days when the fever tick epidemic almost wiped out all of the Florida cattle." The fever tick epidemic dates to the early 1900s and lasted through the 1960s. The tick was responsible for transmitting southern cattle fever. In the 1900s, the southern tick fever was introduced to Florida from Texas and cost the cattle industry upward of $10 million annually. In 1923, the USDA implemented a mandatory cattle dipping program to prevent the spread of the disease.

Since Florida was open range until the late '40s and '50s, when there were no fence laws, cattle roamed freely. When the tick epidemic occurred, cattle ranchers had to build concrete vats containing arsenic formulas to dip cattle in to kill tick eggs and ticks. Griffin the III recalled the hard work he had to endure alongside every family rancher, young and old. "We had to gather up the entire herd every fourteen to twenty-one days and get them into concrete dipping vats which contained 'dope' chemicals and arsenic. When I was six or seven years old, I put cows in the dipping vats. You had to make sure the cow went under all the way, including the head and eyes; then they walked out the concrete vat onto ridges. They were painted with a colored stripe to show they had been dipped. This was a major battle for the cattle industry."

More than 3,400 cattle vats were constructed throughout Florida. The vats were usually twenty-five to thirty feet long, seven feet deep and about three feet wide. Range riders were hired by the government to bring in unmarked cattle or shoot them if the owners could not be identified. Deer, gopher tortoises and other wildlife carried the infected ticks. Long fence lines were built to keep wildlife out and avoid contaminating the dipped cattle.

After surviving the tick epidemic, ranchers were again confronted with a battle against the invasive screwworm. In the 1930s, ranchers had to battle the fly population. When the male and female flies mated, the female would lay eggs in any open wound found on wildlife, cattle or humans. The eggs would then hatch into flesh-eating larvae called screwworms. Ranchers had to fight the screwworms by separating wounded animals from the herd, especially young, newborn calves, as they were the most vulnerable (flies would lay eggs in their unhealed navels). Cattle had to be inspected often, and wounded animals had to be tied down and treated with a repellent of benzol and pine tar oil that at first seemed effective. Later, scientists developed a remedy called Smear 62.

In 1933, the screwworms concentrated in the Southeast and became a threat to humans as well. Female flies would lay eggs in any open wound, and humans could be infested through their noses and sinus cavities. Cattle had to be monitored for any cuts from running into barbed wire, branding or birthing. Entomologists at the USDA's chief scientific research agency, the Agriculture Research Service (ARS), Edward F. Knipling and Raymond C. Bushland tackled the problem. With many trial-and-error methods, they eventually developed a sterile insect technique (SIT), exposing male flies to low doses of atomic radiation that prevented them from reproducing.

The hatching of the screwworm was part of a twenty-one-day cycle in warm weather. If wounds were not treated, the eggs would develop into larvae that "screwed into the flesh of warm blooded animals, feeding on living tissue and fluid." The wound would attract more flies, and if not treated, the host would die. After the screwworm had eaten enough flesh, it would drop onto the ground, burrow itself into the soil and develop into a pupal stage. It would then morph into a fly, and the cycle would continue.

In 1951, large-scale testing was initiated on Sanibel Island, Florida, and it was partially successful. But as it turned out, the island was too close to the mainland, resulting in reinfestation. In 1953, a test was conducted in the Dutch West Indies on the Island of Curaçao, off the coast of Venezuela. After many months and three fly generations, the test was successful, resulting in the complete elimination of the native screwworm population across the entire island. When sterile male flies mated with the females, the females did not lay eggs.

In 1992, the USDA introduced the screwworm eradication program into the Americas, where screwworms were endemic, in order to prevent possible reintroduction into the United States. In 1995, the SIT technique was estimated to benefit U.S. producers in excess of $89 million annually and was the most successful government program in Florida (www.ars.usda.gov).

Despite the area's epidemics and pestilence, many old-time ranchers enjoyed passing the time practicing family traditions, such as square dancing. Griffin III said:

> As a kid, I learned to square dance from Delbert Lowe, and now, I call square dances. Once a year at our ranch, we have a big square dance with two hundred employees and guests. We cook steaks like they did in the old days and prepare a meal like the cow hunters ate on the trail, consisting of black eyed peas, rice, stewed tomatoes, and "pan bread" made from flour and cornmeal cooked in an iron skillet. It is lighter than cornbread, and we have white or salt bacon.

When cow hunters lived on the trail, they had very little to eat, so they loaded up on fat and whatever they could put in their saddle bags to last on the prairie for two or three days. They would take a sweet potato, biscuits and cowboy coffee. (To make cowboy coffee, you pour cold water over the grounds and then pour off the coffee, with the grounds staying at the bottom.) "After working hard all day, the cowboys were tired and hungry, and they always made a big meal at the end of the day." explained Griffin. With large ranch corporations and farms dominating agriculture in Florida, Griffin believes "that small family-owned ranches and farms will stay in business by choice, not economic gain. It is a way of life, and no one should be forced to sell to developers. We are a large corporation, but we are also a family organization."

*Ben Hill Griffin's biography from* The Legacy of the Florida Pioneer Cow Hunters *is used with permission from the author Nancy Dale.*

*The following profiles are shared with permission of the Florida Cattlemen's Foundation. These articles have appeared in monthly editions of the* Florida Cattleman and Livestock Journal, *written by Bob Stone, and were commissioned by the Florida Cattlemen's Foundation in its mission to preserve the history and culture of the Florida beef cattle industry.*

## *Pete Clemons*

Pete Clemons was arguably the most renowned Florida rodeo cowboy of his era. From 1951 to 1955, he won best all around honors at the Silver Spurs Rodeo, the largest rodeo in the East, a record eight times. "He wasn't just an athlete, he was an acrobat!" declared Indiantown rancher Iris Wall. However, there is much more to Pete's story than his stellar rodeo career.

As owner-operator of the Okeechobee Livestock Market, he built the business to be one of the largest markets east of the Mississippi. In the process of growing the business, he did much to help make the Florida beef cattle industry a significant force in the highly competitive modern marketplace. Along the way, he helped many ranchers—large and small—be more competitive in the marketplace and assisted them when they struggled through tough economic times or other misfortune. Osceola County cattleman Lee Radebaugh summed it up nicely: "Pete and his family are just an outstanding bunch of people. Their word is their bond, and I think that's the key to their success. Regardless if you were new to the business or had been in it for generations, they have always been there for everybody. As a young man coming up, Pete was a mentor and counselor for me, as was my grandfather Cushman Radebaugh Sr. It's just been a wonderful relationship and a very real part of my life."

Pete was a fourth-generation Floridian. Born on May 30, 1927, in Kissimmee, Florida, he died at his home in Okeechobee on September 16, 2018. Named Otis Odell Clemons at birth, the man we know as Pete was the second of four children to Oscar and Theresa Bronson Clemons. Oscar and his family were living in Orange County when enumerated in the 1880 U.S. census. Oscar Clemons worked as a cowhand for Irlo Bronson and later became a successful cattleman himself. Pete grew up working his father's ranch. "He had a big place in Brighton; initially, there were three partners," recalled Pete. Oscar Clemons produced Okeechobee's first rodeo, which was held on the Okeechobee Livestock Market grounds. Pete played baseball and football in high school and began competing in rodeos when he was fifteen. Almost from the beginning, Pete specialized in best all around, which entailed competing in five events: bull riding, bareback broncs, saddle broncs, steer wrestling and calf roping.

As a young man, Pete competed in rodeos throughout Florida and the nation. With his rodeo earnings, he worked his way through the University of Florida, graduating with a bachelor of science degree in 1950. Pete traveled to South America twice to serve as an ambassador of U.S. Rodeo. Amazingly, he never broke a bone in twenty-five years of competition.

When the Kissimmee Jaycees asked Pete to represent them at a national convention rodeo in Colorado Spring in 1949, they fixed up a pickup truck to look like a chuck wagon. Artist Buster Kenton decorated it with a cartoon character he named Cowboy Jake. Pete won best all around to the dismay of his western competitors. Cowboy Jake became the mascot for Osceola High School and remains so today.

The Okeechobee Livestock Market was built in the 1930s by the Dixie Cattlemen's Association. It was conveniently located next to the railway, which provided the common mode of transportation for shipping cattle at that time. In August 1948, it was purchased by Robert and Jim Robertson of Wachula, who repaired and modernized the facility. In 1961, Pete bought Okeechobee Livestock Market, partnering with his dad and Quillie Hazellief. Since that time, the market has become Florida's largest market and remains one of the largest volume dealers east of the Mississippi. During the 1980s, it would run 3,000 head of cattle a week, and it continued to average 2,500 per week into the twenty-first century. In 2005, Pete bought out his partners, and today, he and his sons Todd and Jeff run the market. In addition to the traditional marketing approach, the Clemonses utilize innovative video auctions and internet marketing to help bring buyers and sellers together. The family also owns the North Florida Livestock Market in Lake City, managed by grandson Casey.

Pete contributed his time and expertise to many industry and community organizations, including serving as the director of the Okeechobee County Cattlemen's Association, a member of the Farm Bureau, a member of the president's council of the University of Florida, a chairman of the Florida Beef Council, the president of Florida Livestock Markets, a charter member of the National Cattlemen's Association, a member First United Methodist Church, the director of the Federal Land Bank Association and in a number of positions in numerous other organizations.

Pete and his wife, Susanne, and their sons realize the value of philanthropy and charitable support of the community. "The more you give, the more you get back. It's that simple," stated Susanne. "And you can't take it with you." Pete is also known for his personal support of beef cattle producers, large and small. Lee Radebaugh added, "There is no telling what Pete has done behind the scenes for people. He's been the man behind the scenes who put his money where his mouth was. He was there for young people to use as a model. He is an example for anyone to aspire to."

When Okeechobee first celebrated the National Day of the American Cowboy in 2007, Pete was appointed the Big Boss (a sort of grand marshal) of the event, an honor that reflected the high regard for him by his peers. In 2009, he received the Florida Department of State's Folk Heritage Award in recognition of his successful rodeo career at the state, national and international levels and his contributions to the state's cattle ranching community. In 2013, he was inducted into the Florida Sports Hall of Fame, the only rodeo competitor to receive that honor.

Pete Clemons definitely left this world a better place, and we were blessed to have had him working in Florida's cattle industry on all levels. On Pete Clemon's gravestone is an inscription from Ecclesiastes 1:4: "One generation passes and another generation cometh but the land abideth forever." Through a land conservation easement, Pete's son Todd was able to preserve the family's land in perpetuity, fulfilling his dad's last wishes for the land to be saved.

## Stanlo Johns

Stanlo Johns is a valued member of the Seminole cattle program who has worked tirelessly to shape it into a progressive, modern operation. In addition to serving nearly forty years as reservation coordinator of the Cattle and Range Program at the Brighton Seminole Reservation, he served a term as president of the Glades County Cattlemen's Association. In recognition of his contributions as a leader in cattle ranching and environmental stewardship, the Chalo Nika Festival Committee honored him as the grand marshal of the seventieth anniversary festival in 2018. A proud member of the Panther Clan, he is dedicated to the preservation and continuity of his Native language and culture.

According to oral history, the Johns family of Seminole Indians lived in the St. Johns River Basin in the nineteenth century—and quite possibly earlier—pointing to the root of their English language surname. Among their most renowned ancestors is Coacoochee (Ko AH koo chee), also known as Wild Cat, who was a significant leader in the Second Seminole War (1835–42). The date and place of Wild Cat's birth are not clear, but he was probably born near the St.

Stanlo Johns. *Bob Stone.*

Johns River between 1808 and 1816. His uncle was Micanopy (or Micco Nuppa), the micco, or head chief, of the entire Seminole Confederation. His father, Emathia (King Phillip), was the micco of Seminoles in towns along the St. Johns River, which comprised a major portion of the Seminole Confederation.

Wild Cat was a clever, fierce warrior and talented leader. A large number of Black people, many of whom had fled slavery in the southern states and territories, lived in Florida with the Seminoles. While they were considered enslaved, in actual practice, the Black Seminoles lived as feudal serfs, residing in their own settlements and paying the local Seminole leader a tribute in the form of a percentage of their annual crops. While intermarriage between the Seminole and Black populations was not commonplace, it did occur.

Stanlo Johns was born on July 4, 1935, in his family's camp in the Bluefield area, north of Indiantown at the border of Martin and St. Lucie Counties. His family was one of many Seminole families who lived in the area surrounding Indiantown, which was a trading center. At that time, all the Indians lived on land owned by private parties, the State of Florida or the United States government. With the establishment of the Brighton Reservation near the northwest side of Lake Okeechobee in 1935–38, Stanlo's family and the other Muskogee (or Creek)-speaking Seminoles scattered throughout the region moved there. He recalled that some of his uncles who visited his family at the Brighton Reservation would not stay overnight because they were afraid the reservation was a plot to get all the Seminoles in one place so they could be shipped to Indian Territory in Oklahoma.

In 1938, at the request of the Brighton Seminole leaders, the U.S. Department of Indian Affairs hired the husband-and-wife team of Mr. and Mrs. William D. Boehmer to teach school and engage in community development work. In 1939, a school constructed by the Civilian Conservation Corps–Indian Division opened. Stanlo and most of the children his age spoke only the Creek language. At the new school, they studied English and other subjects. When he reached the third grade, Stanlo, along with several other reservation children around his age, attended a boarding school in Cherokee, North Carolina, for about six months of the year. This separation from his family was a painful ordeal for young Stanlo. "She just sent me off," Stanlo said. Ultimately, he adjusted to life at the boarding school and realized the importance of learning English. "I just made up my mind: 'I've got to learn this English.'"

After about three years of boarding school, Stanlo's parents enrolled him in the sixth grade in the Okeechobee Public School System. There, he met

Jonnie Rhoden, whom he married in 1960. Stanlo and Jonnie had three children, Kay, Jeff and Todd.

The Seminoles and their ancestors have a long history of cattle ranching. During the Spanish colonial period, Natives worked as cowhands for the Spanish. After the British-Creek invasions destroyed the Spanish ranchos in 1702 and 1704, the Cow Creeks, as white people called the Natives at the time, grazed large herds in present-day Alachua County and elsewhere. The Johns family are descendants of Cowkeeper, who owned as many as seven to ten thousand head of cattle that grazed around the Indian settlement of Cuscowilla in the Alachua Prairie Basin, near Gainesville.

The establishment of the Brighton Reservation ushered in the modern era of Seminole cattle ranching. In 1936, during the New Deal era, the U.S. government shipped 547 head of Hereford cattle from the southwestern Dust Bowl to the railhead of Cornwell, about eighteen miles north of the Brighton Reservation. Many of the undernourished cattle died en route to Cornwell, and still more died on the drive to Brighton, but the surviving stock provided the core of the growing herd. Fred Montsdeoca, an Okeechobee County agricultural agent, worked with Brighton cattlemen to bring them into self-sufficiency.

Drafted into the U.S. Army when he was eighteen, Stanlo achieved a specialist 4 rank during his two years of service. When he returned to Florida, he landed a job as cattle foreman of Brighton. Stanlo acquired his first cattle in 1959. Having worked closely with Fred Montsdeoca for many years, he said, "If it wasn't for him, the Seminole tribe would not have what they have today. He's the one who united the cattlemen together and showed them what they needed to do and how to do it."

Together, Stanlo and Fred established a successful cooperative cattle program. Today, the sixty-eight cattle owners in the program are required to have a herd of at least seventy-five head. Each owner is allotted pasture acreage commensurate to the size of their herd and pay a grazing fee to cover the costs of working and caring for the cattle. The program gives its participants the advantage of uniform, centralized management and economy of scale for medicine and other expenses. Since the calves produced by the program's members are of uniform quality, they are sold by video auction, saving the cost and stress of transporting them to a livestock market. The Seminole tribe was one of the first beef cattle producers in the state to institute a program of 100 percent electronic ID.

Today, the tribe successfully manages five operations: the Brighton Reservation and Big Cypress Reservation Board Cattle I, II and III.

Combined, there are more than twelve thousand head of cattle (tribal and individual) grazing on 38,200 acres of native and improved pastures. Over the years, the tribe has raised several different breeds of cattle, including Brangus, Hereford, Braford and Beefmaster. The Seminole tribe of Florida, as of this writing, ranks fourth in the state in cow-calf production and twelfth in the nation.

Former Florida Cattlemen's Association president Alex Johns (also Stanlo's cousin) expressed deep appreciation for Stanlo's contributions to modern Seminole cattle operations. "Stanlo was an integral part of the Seminoles' progress in cattle production," stated Alex.

*He grew up in an era when Creek was his first language, but he also learned English at an early age and was the go-to interpreter for the older Seminoles. This gave him an advantage in life to bridge both worlds, and fueled his entrepreneurial spirit. He also had an inherent ability to understand cattle and possessed some unique skills. For instance, he can cut more than sixty-seven different earmarks and makes an art out of his earmark designs. He has been a great mentor to me, not only in cattle, but in business as well.*

Realizing the role language plays in cultural preservation and continuity, Stanlo is a passionate advocate for teaching the Creek language to young people. Through his participation in the Teaching the Teachers program at the Pemayetv Emahakv Charter School, he works with teachers to instruct them in the Creek language so they can correctly instruct their students.

Stanlo and his sons formed the highly respected Johns Family Enterprises LLC, which Jeff and Todd run. Stanlo and Jonnie, his wife of fifty-eight years, are enjoying an active retirement. With the assistance of his sons, Stanlo continues to tend his herd of more than two hundred head of cattle, and he and Jonnie cherish the time they spend with their grandchildren.

## *Payne Midyette Jr.*

In 1706, the ancestors of Payne Midyette Jr. (pronounced Mid-jet) sailing from Canada to New Orleans became shipwrecked off the coast of Cape Hatteras, North Carolina, and, as a result, settled there. Payne Midyette Sr. moved from North Carolina in 1922 and formed the Midyette-Moor Insurance Company with a partner and also raised cattle. Payne Midyette Jr. was born on August 13, 1927, in Tallahassee, Florida. For as long as he could remember, he helped his father with the family cattle. His passion for raising cattle remained strong. At an early age, Payne showed a talent for caring for cattle and a good business sense. "When I was a kid, I used to buy old piney woods cows that everybody was selling, because the price was so good. I would bring them to pasture in my dad's truck, deworm them with a drench, put them on a good pasture, and in about ninety days, I'd take them back to the market and sell them. I'd make spending money as a kid that way."

In 1940, Alto L. Adams of Fort Pierce was appointed as a Florida Supreme Court judge. When he relocated his family to Tallahassee, Payne quickly became close friends with Judge Adams's son Alto Jr., known as Bud. "Bud and I rode our horses all over the southern part of Leon and Wakulla Counties, camping and exploring," recalled Payne. "We worked in the summertime for Mr. Irlo Bronson. He was one of the great cattlemen of his time and a wonderful mentor. It was a great experience. I had a good time and learned a lot." Payne and Bud remained lifelong friends.

After graduating from Leon High School, Payne joined the U.S. Navy Seabees during the latter part of World War I and was stationed in Rhode Island, Oahu, Hawaii and several other locations in the South Pacific. The war soon ended, and he was discharged on his nineteenth birthday, August 13, 1946. He subsequently enrolled in the University of Florida and graduated with a degree in agriculture economics.

Payne then went to work for Bud Adams and his father at the Adams Ranch in Fort Pierce. Payne enjoyed the work and wanted to live in South Florida, but fate intervened when he injured his back riding a bucking bull in a rodeo. Unable to ride a horse for ranch work, he moved back to Tallahassee, where it took him a year to recover.

Payne formed a partnership with his father and took over the management of his purebred Hereford cattle. He married Jean Jarrett in 1951, and they had three children: Payne III, Alma Jane "Janie" and Aren. As a family man with growing responsibilities, in 1951, he realized he was not earning enough money in the cattle business to support his family. He sold some of his cattle and reluctantly went to work for the Midyette-Moor Insurance Agency. "I really didn't want to do that, but it turned out to be something I thoroughly enjoyed. And I did a good job at it. Midyette-Moor went on to become one of the top insurance companies in Florida." Payne continued to run the agency until he retired in 1992.

During his time working with the insurance agency, he continued to raise cattle, albeit on a reduced scale. "We bought our first Braford cattle from Bud Adams in 1981—4 bulls and 125 heifers," recalled Payne. After his retirement from the insurance business, he ramped up his cattle operation. He had two groups of cattle on his Running M Ranch, located between Madison and Greenville: a Braford herd and a mixed red Angus and Braford commercial herd.

Payne was given a Cracker horse by his good friend Okeechobee veterinarian Dr. Jim Harvey, who is also a Braford breeder. "Jim sent me a little Cracker filly," Payne said. "Because I didn't charge him enough for a bull I had sold him. I also had a really nice Cracker stud we called Pretty Boy, and we started riding Cracker horses to work the ranch, and that's what we ride today." He was also a member of the Cracker Horse Association and an active participant on many trail rides with the group. One of his greatest joys was having his daughters, Mary Hill and Aren, and granddaughters Rebecca and Catherine share his love of horses and riding when they accompanied him on trail rides. In 2006, he won an award as the oldest rider and continued to ride his horses until he was eighty-seven.

Payne operated the Running M Ranch with the help of his grandson Will Moncrief (Aren's son), veteran cowboy Kit Storey and horse trainer Jake Bentley, who helped out part time. Raising cattle in the eastern panhandle differs considerably from cattle ranching in the southern part of the state. "If we have a hard frost, we won't have green grass until next spring," explained Payne. "Down south, it will green back up again. They feed a little hay down south, we feed a lot. So, it costs more to raise cattle here." Kit added, "I am either bailing hay or feeding it."

Throughout his decades of cattle ranching, Payne maintained a passion for the Braford breed. He was the last president of the old International Braford Association (IBA). He then brought the American Braford Association and the United Braford Association together to form the United Braford Breeders (UBB) in 1994, and he served as its first elected president. At the annual membership meeting in Houston, Texas, in 2012, he was honored by the UBB with the Robert R. Buescher Memorial Award, the UBB's highest honor for persons who have made significant contributions to the UBB and/ or beef cattle seedstock industry. In the spring 2012 issue of the *Braford News*, the UBB noted:

> *Payne has served as a wise and steady force on the UBB Board of Directors for years and was recently elected for another term. The UBB's Performance*

*Opposite*: Iris Wall and Celina Murray Moncrief. *Karen Howard.*

*Left*: Payne Midyett and his grandson Will Moncrief riding Cracker horses. *Midyette family.*

*Breeder of the Year award was named after him and he continues to be a leader in producing performance-oriented registered Brafords appreciated and utilized in a number of breeding programs throughout the U.S. as well as internationally. His efforts also focused on the establishment of a registered Braford herd at the University of Florida research station in Marianna, Florida. He made a significant donation of registered cows to establish that herd with the stipulation that they maintain them as registered Brafords with full performance reporting.*

Like many of his generation, Payne readily acknowledged he owed a great debt to geneticist Dr. Marvin Koger and reproductive physiology professor Dr. Alvin Warnick of the Universtiy of Florida. "Those two men probably did more to improve Florida cattle than anyone. Both of them were super scientists." Payne was also an enthusiastic supporter of the Florida Cattlemen's Foundation in its mission to support research, education and leadership development and to preserve Florida's ranching history and heritage.

Payne Midyette Jr. died on Easter Sunday, April 4, 2021, surrounded by his family and faithful cow dog Buddy. His grandson Will and Will's wife, Celina Murray Moncrief, have taken over the operation of the ranch. "Will is a hard worker and very smart," Payne declared of his grandson. Although there will be many challenges to operating the Running M Ranch, Payne believed his grandson up to the task. "There is still opportunity out there. It is not opportunity the way I remember it, but it's there. These younger people are pretty adaptable to all this technology, and that's where it's going to come from."

## Iris Wall

Iris Wall's life is a love story. She loved her husband, Homer, through forty-seven years of marriage. "I had the best husband in the world," she beamed. "I was crazy about him, and he loved me the same way." She loves cow hunting, and she loves Florida. "There's nobody in the state of Florida who loves it more than I do," she declared. Iris also loves children and has taken numerous groups of schoolchildren on field trips around her ranch, teaching them the history of old Florida and about the importance of caring for the land and water. She has more friends than she can count. "I wouldn't take nothin' for all the friends I have. People have been so good to me. God has been so good to me. I've had a wonderful life."

She was born November 23, 1929, at the start of the Great Depression, to Cecil and Lois Roland Pollack. "Times were hard, but we got along somehow. If we were poor, we didn't know it. We had everything we needed," Iris stated. Her mother's family, the Rolands, were numerous, with deep roots in Florida, and they figured significantly in the history of Indiantown. According to Iris, the Roland family originated in Abbeville, Alabama. In 1870, the U.S. census counted her maternal great-grandfather Roland and his wife, Susan, as living in Alachua County. Her grandfather Alonzo Roland married Anna Smith in Alachua County in 1896, and they settled in Indiantown around 1920.

Indiantown was a major trading hub for Seminoles who lived in the area before the Brighton and Big Cypress Reservations were established in the 1930s. Many of the Indians traded at the store and trading post operated by Joe Bowers. "In those days, if you were from Indiantown, you were either 'Uncle' or 'Aunt,'" recalled Iris. "Uncle Joe Bowers was close with the Indians. They planted his grove." By 1925, Iris's grandmother had bought some land in Indiantown, where she also operated the U.S. Post Office and served as postmaster. Iris developed personal relationships with many of the Seminoles—she and Betty Mae Tiger Jumper, the only female leader of the Seminole tribe of Florida from 1967 to 1971, were especially close and maintained a friendship until Betty's death in 1987.

Iris grew up cow hunting in the days of the open range. "I just pure loved to cow hunt!" she exclaimed. "Our pasture ran clean from Indiantown to Palm City. They'd gather about one hundred cows and put us young 'uns in charge to hold 'em. The men communicated to us by cracking the whips." She usually rode all day long, working cows until dark. In her saddle pockets, she carried strips of white bacon (called fatback) and maybe a sweet potato for dinner. They drank pond water and cooked over open fires. Frequently, she rode with Joe Bowers. "I've cow-hunted with Uncle Joe day after day after day." During the 1940s, she worked seemingly endlessly, roping calves and cows and doctoring them for screwworms.

Iris met the love of her life, Homer Wall, at Warfield School in Indiantown. "When we were in the sixth grade, we put on a play called *Drusilla's Garden*. I was Aunt Drusilla, and Homer was the gardener. I fell in love with the gardener and loved him for the rest of his life." Homer was a cow hunter, and most folks called him Cowboy, a moniker that stuck with him for life.

Iris Wall, age fifteen, on Cracker horse "Bull." *Iris Wall.*

Before electric lights, running water or telephones came to the woods of South Florida, folks provided their own entertainment. Iris recalled many evenings when the men would crack cow whips out in Grandma Roland's yard, sometimes asking Iris or one of her sisters to hold a matchstick in her teeth while one of them skillfully popped it from the girl's mouth. "They were masters with those big 'ol fifteen-foot cow whips!" Iris declared. Folks used cow whips for communication, too; its loud crack can be heard for about two miles. "If Grandma wanted us, she'd just pop that whip three times, and we'd come." Another form of entertainment was the frolic, or community dance. "Over at Grandma's, they'd push all the furniture back out of the way and square dance in the living room and dining room. One of Grandma's friends, Ran Smith, played the fiddle, and his sons, Clyde, Paul and Jesse, played mouth-harps [harmonicas] and guitar." Iris remembered that they would improvise some sort of drum, using something to create a beat on the floor, like a broomstick. Uncle Rand called the dance figures.

In 1949, it became mandatory to fence cattle rangeland. The new law put many cattlemen who grazed their cattle on the open range out of business. Those who continued ranching had to build fences on the land they owned or leased. Recognizing an economic opportunity, Iris's father, Cecil Pollock, went into the business of meeting the tremendous demand for posts to fence thousands upon thousands of acres of rangeland. Members of the Durrance family of pioneering cattlemen were among his major clients. From 1955 to 1959, Iris and Homer Wall camped at the end of Oil Well Grade, west of Immokalee near the Corkscrew Swamp. Homer worked for his father-in-law, cutting young cypress trees for ten cents per post. There were no chainsaws then; he cut every post with an axe. "Homer was about six foot, one, a great, big, strong, healthy guy," beamed Iris. "He could cut a tree with three licks of an axe—two on one side and one on the other—he brought a tree down, "He always cut two hundred a day. A semi could hold one thousand posts, and when he had cut a semi load, he would load one thousand posts that same night, after cutting all day." Iris and Homer had no electricity, running water or plumbing at the camp. Their daughter Terry was three months old when they moved there, and in 1953, Iris gave birth to their second daughter, Jonnie. Despite their total lack of amenities, the young family enjoyed life in the swamp.

Homer hunted alligators to supplement their income during the early years of their lives. "When you work for $150 a month and you can get $35 for a five-foot alligator, you know darn well you're going gator hunting. That's how we bought many pairs of shoes." While Homer and some men were fencing a large plot that is now the J.W. Corbett Wildlife Management Area, they discovered a pond full of big alligators. After they had killed several alligators and skinned them, Iris noticed an airplane making repeated passes overhead. Because it was illegal, gator hunters were always on the lookout for game wardens and she told Homer the game warden would probably arrive in a few minutes. Homer and the men quickly stashed the alligator hides in a large wooden box on the bed of a wagon they used for hauling fencing materials. Homer then directed Iris to sit on the box and not get up no matter what. "I was sittin' on that box and not getting' off no matter what. I was sittin' on that box right out in the bald open," she recalled. Soon, Officer Jimmy Lanier arrived. Jimmy asked, "What are you boys doing?" Homer replied, "Just buildin' fence."

"Well, Jimmy kept talkin' and talkin', and I just set there in the broilin' sun. After a bit, he began to walk around lookin' at this and lookin' at that, and there I was, out in the broilin' sun, sweat just pourin' off me. This went on and on and on. I prayed he would not ask me to get up and move. After a while, he just hit on the edge of that box and said, 'Now, you boys be careful and don't you get caught,' and walked off." Throughout their lives, Jimmy Lanier and Iris laughed over the incident many times.

With a contact through church, Homer went to work for a company called Air Products and quickly advanced through the ranks. He was then transferred to Cape Canaveral, where he worked for a plant that made fuel for rockets and witnessed the launch of John Glenn's rocket, the Friendship 7. Homer and Iris soon found their way back to Indiantown, where they invested in a lumberyard, which eventually expanded to include five combination W&W Lumber Yards and Ace Hardware Stores. They also bought the historic Seminole Inn, built by railroad tycoon Solomon Davies Warfield in 1949, which their daughter Jonnie operates today.

Sadly, Homer died in 1994. His passing was devastating for Iris, but her strong Christian faith enabled her to survive her loss and continue to love life. Reflecting on her beloved Homer, Iris said, "Most people love money and use people. Homer loved people and used money."

Iris is active in Indiantown community life and in the state cattle ranching community. For years, she hosted field trips to her High Horse Ranch for public schoolchildren. She has been an active member and officer in both the Cracker Cattle and Cracker Horse Associations, hosting annual meetings and gatherings at her ranch. Commissioner Charles Bronson honored her with the 2006 Woman of the Year in Agriculture award for her lifetime of work in cattle ranching, preserving heritage breeds and participating in conservation and education. Iris has set demonstration cow camps annually at the Florida Cattlemen's Foundation's Ranch Rodeo and Cowboy Heritage Festival. In 2010, she traveled to the Western Folklife Center in Elko, Nevada, where she, Buddy Mills and his wife, Jessie, delighted participants with a Cracker cooking workshop titled "Put a Little South in Your Mouth." The Florida Cattle Ranching exhibit was on display there during the national Cowboy Poetry Gathering. A variety of nonprofit organizations wish for her to present her engaging presentations of "Tales of Cracker Life." Wherever she travels, Iris is a warm-hearted and engaging ambassador for Florida cattle ranching and Cracker traditions. She loves people and wins friends instantly.

Today, Iris raises a herd of cross-bred cattle on her 1,265-acre ranch and a small herd of Cracker cattle near her home on Little Ranch Estates in Indiantown. Her family all pitch in to work with the cattle. Although she has been rewarded with material wealth as a result of her decades of hard work and honest dealing, Iris realizes there is much more to life. "The most successful position in the world is to be satisfied, and you know I'm satisfied." And she offers this advice: "If you don't own but one acre of land, keep it green. Try and take care of it. Be a keeper of the land."

A class field trip to High Horse Ranch. *Author's collection.*

Wagon ride around High Horse Ranch. *Author's collection.*

Cracker calves. *Iris Wall.*

*Opposite, top*: Pumping water the old-fashioned way. *Author's collection.*

*Opposite, bottom*: Climbing on bales of hay. *Author's collection.*

*Above*: Washing clothes in a washtub. *Author's collection.*

*Left*: Cow whip popping practice. *Author's collection.*

*Left*: Ironing the old-fashioned way. *Author's collection.*

*Right*: Lassoing practice. *Author's collection.*

## Imogene Yarborough

Imogene Yarborough was born Barbara Imogene Bostick on August 2, 1935, in Ocala, Florida, and passed away on April 24, 2023. Her mother's family raised cattle in Sumter County, and in 1949, her stepfather moved the family to Geneva so he could work with his brother in the cattle business. In Geneva, Imogene met Ed Yarborough, whose grandfather E.H. Kilbee ran a large cattle ranch there. Ed and Imogene were married in 1954 and had two daughters and two sons: Lynn, Bo, J.W. and Reba.

Ed's uncle and aunt W.G. and Katherine Kilbee died in a tragic automobile accident while traveling home from a cattlemen's meeting in 1969. They had no children, and Ed and his sisters inherited the Kilbee family's twelve-thousand-acre ranch.

Ed Yarborough earned a reputation as an expert cowman dedicated to the Florida beef cattle industry and the well-being of Seminole County. He had plenty of cow sense and showed great talent in uniting cows and calves that had somehow been separated from each other. "Ed was good at reading earmarks and very good at 'mammying up' cows [matching cows with their calves]," stated Imogene. "He had a really good memory for cows." He served as president of the Seminole County Cattlemen's Association for twelve years. The Florida Cattlemen's Association made him an honorary member in 1999. Following in the footsteps of E.H. and W.G. Kilbee, who had both been county commissioners, Ed served two consecutive terms as Seminole County Commissioner from 1964 to 1972.

Ed and Imogene's sons, Bo and J.W., learned a lot from their father, and they, in turn, continue to pass their knowledge and skills to their progeny. J.W.'s son C.W. works on the ranch with his father and uncle Bo, and his brother J.K., the fourth generation of his family to graduate from the University of Florida, serves as an extension agent for livestock/natural resources for Orange and Seminole Counties. Bo's son Robert, a senior ranger with the State Fire Service and top-notch cowboy, is a valued member of the family ranch crew.

After Ed died in 2000, J.W. and Bo worked hard to improve their cow/calf operation. By using upgraded bulls, taking better care of their cattle and practicing an improved medicine regimen, they achieved a substantial increase in their calf weight. Imogene embraces technology and makes the most of change. "Mom has done a great job adapting," stated Bo. "She has always had an open mind."

The Yarborough Ranch is a family operation that uses very little outside help. Imogene and her daughters-in-law, Beverly and Francis, pitch in to help with the ranch work, doing whatever it takes to get the job done. While still a high school student, Lynn worked on the ranch early in the morning, before her first class began. She embarked on a demanding career of teaching children with learning disabilities in 1979 but continued to help at the ranch as her schedule permitted.

It would take several pages to list Imogene's accomplishments and honors. Some highlights on the national level include her reception of the National Farm City Award (1983), her past service as the director of the National Cattlewomen's Association, her seven years of service as a committee member for the National Beef Cookoff and her service as the first Florida Cattlewomen's Association president. In 2007, she and Ed were inducted into the Florida Agriculture Hall of Fame; in 2012, she was named woman of the year in agriculture; and in 2018, the University of Florida Institute for Agricultural Sciences honored her with the Extension Advocate Award.

Imogene "Mamagene" Yarborough, Woman of the Year in Agriculture. *Florida Archives.*

"The Farm Bureau has been dear to my heart," declared Imogene. "It has always had the most pleasant, knowledgeable young men and women." Her service to the Seminole County Farm Bureau includes terms as president (2000–2006), vice-president (1994–99), secretary (1986–87), treasurer (2007–present) and a member of the board of directors (1984–present).

Imogene was humble about all the awards she has received. "I didn't even know some of these awards existed until I got the call. I've gone out to educate people about what our world is about." One of Imogene's favorite activities was educating children about the many uses of beef. She strongly believes in the importance of teaching people about agriculture. To celebrate Florida's rich history of cattle ranching and to increase public awareness, Imogene has helped organize all four Great Florida Cattle Drives, serving as treasurer and chairperson for the ways and means committee, and she was a founding member of the Florida Agricultural Museum. In 2022, she attended the Great Florida Cattle Drive that marked the five hundredth anniversary of horses and cattle in Florida. There, the following story was told by Jim McAllistar about her expert dog handling skills.

*Crackers are known for getting a job done no matter what it takes. They will overcome any obstacle, work through any problem, and if need be, create entirely new ways of doing things all in the name of seeing the day's work through. This brings to mind just such an incident that happened many years ago on the Yarborough ranch in Geneva. It should be noted that I was not present for this story, but rather, it was told to me by Miss Imogene herself, and I will attempt to relay it to you in as accurate detail possible.*

*The time had come to move a group of cattle up to the pens to be worked. Mr. Ed Yarborough and the boys went about the normal routine of collecting supplies, saddling horses, and gathering dogs and set out for the day's work. Miss Imogene, being the dutiful ranch wife, remained at home to tend to the duties around the house. Once she was done, she would head to the pens to meet up with Ed and the crew, bring them lunch, and assist with whatever work needed to be done. Like most Florida cattle ranchers, they made use of dogs when it came to working cattle. While Ed and the boys had taken a group of dogs with them that morning, they left their best dog Jip behind. Jip was the finest of cow dogs, able to turn back the rankest most stubborn bovine. She was a true asset when it came to moving a herd. Jip only had one problem: she had a tendency to work herself right into the ground. Because of this, she was often held in reserve until she was needed.*

"Cowman" license plate belonging to the Yarborough family. *Author's collection.*

*Before leaving Miss Imogene that day, Ed had given her instructions to bring Jip with her when she came out.*

*When the time came, Miss Imogene prepared to make her way to the pens. Now, it just so happened that Miss Imogene was the proud owner of a bright new shiny Crown Victoria. Sleek and beautiful, the interior of the car provided all of the comforts anyone could ever want. This created a problem when it came time to load Jip. No matter how valuable an asset, there was no way Miss Imogene was going to put that dirty cur dog in her nice clean car. But what to do? The dog had to go, and her car was the only means of transportation available. After giving it some thought, Miss Imogene set upon a plan. Rather than put the dog in the passenger compartment of her car, she would simply put it in the trunk. It was only a short drive to her destination, and it would keep her car clean. So, with the dog safely stowed away, off Miss Imogene went.*

*Miss Imogene made her way to the pens, and soon, Ed and the boys came into sight. They were close but had not yet made it to their destination at the cow pens. Now, any good cow hunter, male or female, young or old,* can watch a herd on the move and tell if things are going right. It just so happened that the signs Miss Imogene witnessed that day told her the cattle were not being as cooperative as one might hope. It was as if she could see the wreck developing before it happened and instinctively began to move herself into position to help should she be needed. Sure enough, as the herd reached the pens, it began to break up, and mild chaos ensued. The boys and dogs made their moves to gain control, but their position on the herd made it difficult to get where they needed to be. As if by design, Miss Imogene sprang into action. Pressing down on the accelerator, she gave the car a healthy dose of fuel and began to run for the head of the herd. With rooster tails flying, she began to close the gap between her and the disobedient group of bovine. Ed and the boys were still working to overtake the herd, but it soon became apparent that Miss Imogene had the advantage. After all, each of the boys were only working with one horsepower while Miss Imogene had harnessed 150.

All of this might have been easy enough, but it just so happened that the pasture Miss Imogene was crossing had, at one time, been a citrus grove. Anyone who has ever been in a pasture that has been converted from citrus knows that the ground is not in any way smooth but more closely resembles the texture of a pair of corduroy britches. Driving this ground at slow speeds can be rough enough, I can only imagine the teeth rattling, bone jarring ride that would be created at high speeds. It is safe to say that Henry Ford and his engineers could not have come up with a tougher way to test a car's suspension than that Crown Vic experienced that day.

The whole time this is unfolding, Jip (remember Jip?) was still sequestered to the dark confines of the vehicle's trunk. I can only imagine the thoughts going through the poor dog's mind as it went from being a comfy passenger to something that more closely resembled the K9 equivalent of ice in a martini shaker. The poor critter must have seriously begun to doubt the sanity of the person whose care she had been entrusted.

Using moves that would have made the most seasoned of Hollywood stunt drivers proud, Miss Imogene reached the head of the herd. It just so happened that this particular Crown Vic had a feature in it that would come in particularly handy that day. Positioned on the dashboard was a button that, when pushed, would cause the trunk of the vehicle to open. As Miss Imogene swung the car around in a perfect 180 and positioned herself at the front of the collection of cranky cattle, she reached up…and pushed the button. Instantaneously, the lid of the trunk flew open, and the previously confined cow dog was launched from the rear of the car. Without *missing so much as a single beat, Jip hit the ground running and made for the lead cow. Quick work was made of turning the herd and bringing them back under control. The cow crew was able to place the errant cattle back on the proper path, and they were moved to the pens without further incident.*

*Whether it was Miss Imogene's impressive driving skills, the shock of suddenly being faced with a rather unusual mode of herding apparatus, the judicious placement of a top notch cow dog or a combination of the three that brought the herd under control, it was obvious that not only had Miss Imogene's quick thinking saved the day, but that she was the first and perhaps the only person in Florida cattle history to make use of a rapid deployment cow dog.*

## Preserving the Breeds

### *The Florida Cracker Horse: Florida's Heritage Horse*

*Rare is the person who has never wondered where horses first came from, what person first thought to capture them, and how they were tamed and formed into breeds useful to mankind. Every horseman who ponders these questions, struck by the beauty and uniqueness of his own favorite, is really contemplating a very personal question: "How came my mount, through these long generations, to me?"*
—Deb Bennett, PhD

Many believe, perhaps because they have seen the primitive looking Przewalski horse at a zoo, that this is the ancestor of all the breeds of domestic horses. Its appearance makes it seem, to many people, a perfect candidate for a living fossil. However, the remains of Przewalski horses and even their nearest relatives, the tarpan, Lamut wild horse and American glacial horse, are only some 200,000 years old. The oldest fossils so far discovered that could possibly belong to *Equus caballus* are about 1.4 million years old and come from Nebraska. Fossil bones show that many herds of horses migrated from North America to Eurasia during the ice age.

This animal, *Equus caballus midlandensis*, was the last wild horse ever to exist in North America. In tandem with the last severe glaciation—which pinched its narrow strip of grazing land into a chain of ice-rimmed pockets of Alaska—came the hunter, who knew from experience in Eurasia how to spear horses for food. The once vast herds were driven out of existence because isolated bands could not propagate in great numbers—they had nowhere to go and limited food resources—nor could members of one herd easily reach other herds in order to breed. When hunting reduced their numbers further still, America's last wild horses flickered out. There is more than one way for a species to become extinct—it does not always happen by fang and claw. A subspecies can be made extinct by being taken wholly into domestication. Even horses of the Przewalski group are now extinct in the wild. Today, they exist only in zoos.

Horses were essential to the European conquest of the New World, and the Iberians were lucky; of all the livestock they imported, horses fit into New World biomes, especially temperate latitudes, as if they belonged. Indeed, they do belong, for this is the land of origin of the family Equidae and genus Equus—if not the species *Equus caballus*. Because they were able to occupy—or reoccupy as it were—an apparently empty ecological niche, horses burgeoned nearly everywhere in the New World, so much so that they became feral. The Spanish jennet—that intelligent, noble, handsome, brave and worthy animal—is the one horse that contributed to the ancestry of all horse breeds originating in the Americas.

The story of American horses is a long one. American horses derive from those of Iberia, and the roots of Iberian bloodlines spread across the expanse of the Old World—to Africa, Thrace, Anatolia, Persia, Afghanistan and the Eurasian Steppe. The life of the Iberian horse for the past three thousand years has been bound with the history of civilization—in trade, transportation and war. The characteristics of its American descendants help identify it. The breeds that reflect it most are the Criollos, Coralleros, Baguales, Pasos, Llaneros and more. The type of horse that the conquest delivered to the New World was the jennet—in all its characteristics of temperament, body shape, physiology and gait—and it has primarily been preserved. Over half a millennium, documents Deb Bennet PhD in her book, *Conquerors: The Roots of New World Horsemanship*, it has even been preserved almost without change or adulteration.

The Caribbean's breeding farms supplied the horses needed by the Spanish conquistadors for their explorations and conquests of the New World. They ranged in height from thirteen and a half to fifteen hands, and their general description included a short back, sloping rump, low tail set, good limbs and hooves, wide forehead, beautiful eyes, delicately formed nostrils and sloping shoulders. Based on that description, it appears that the Cracker horse of today obviously shares many of the same characteristics as those horses brought from the Caribbean five hundred years ago.

Cracker horses get their name from the Cracker cow hunters who used them. Over the years, Cracker horses have been known by a variety of names, including the Florida Horse, Marsh Tacky, Seminole Pony, Chickasaw Pony, Prairie Pony, Florida Cow Pony and many others. Like their ancestors, Cracker horses range in height from thirteen and a half to fifteen hands, and their weight runs from about 750 to over 1,000 pounds. They are known for their unusual strength, endurance, herding instincts, quickness and fast walking gait. Some of them have either a single foot or running walk that seems to have been passed on to them by the Spanish jennet. A Cracker horse can be any color common to horses; however, the solid colors and grays are predominant.

During the Florida frontier years and into the twentieth century, the Cracker horse was used for just about anything horses in Florida could be used for—pulling wagons, buggies, sleds, plows and cane mills or taking kids to school—but they were always used as cow ponies. Florida was strategically important to both sides of the Civil War, supplying beef, staple goods and horses. Horses were the backbone of the Civil War. They moved guns and ambulances and carried generals. Over one million horses and mules were killed in battle. Spanish horses were highly prized for their toughness. These sturdy horses of Spanish descent could travel in rough conditions. Today, though they are still used to work cattle, Cracker horses are finding their way into team penning, team roping, trail riding, endurance riding and cutting cattle, and they are used as mounts in historical reenactments.

Herds of escaped Spanish horses were common in Florida until recent times. The breed is now officially known as the Florida Cracker horse, and the Florida legislature adopted it as the official heritage horse of Florida in 2008. Florida's perfect climate for raising cattle and horses provided the near demise of the Florida Cracker horse. In the 1930s, the lush vegetation and ample pastureland beckoned to the drought-stricken Midwest regions during the Great Depression, and livestock were driven there.

The importation of these "foreign" cattle species brought a parasite known as a screwworm, which negatively affected all the livestock, resulting in a loss of overall condition and weight in the state's livestock. To keep the livestock parasite free, it became necessary to rope and hold the new and larger cattle for treatment. This resulted in a trend of using larger and heavier horses to manage the cattle. The original quarter horse was the result of crossing newly imported English Thoroughbreds with local Chickasaw horses in Virginia and the Carolinas. In the Carolinas, the Spanish horses the Indians brought up from the south were called Chickasaw ponies. These horses came from the same bloodlines as the Spanish Cracker horses in Florida. The crossing of these Spanish horses with the English horses yielded a quick and fast "quarter pather." This early quarter horse was also a good cow horse and crowded out the Florida Cracker, which nearly went extinct according to Sam P. Getzen in his article for the *Florida Cracker Horse Association Newsletter*, "Cracker-Florida's Heritage Horses," and Jane Blais in her article "The Forgotten."

Many of the wild Cracker horses died from the screwworms, because they did not receive treatment. The breed's survival today is due to the efforts of a few Florida ranchers who tried to maintain the type and quality of the breed. One rancher named John Law Ayers of Brooksville, Florida, chose not to change the breed in the 1930s and kept his own herd of Cracker horses, as did other small, independent ranchers. In 1984, Ayers donated horses from his Cracker horse herds to the Agricultural Museum in Tallahassee and the Withlacoochee State Forest in Central Florida. Doyle Conner from the Florida Department of Agriculture and Consumer Services Commissioner grew up riding Cracker horses in the open ranges of Bradford and adjoining counties. He and several Florida cattlemen who spent much of their lives on

Pioneer reenactors Azel "Cooter" Nail and Tony "Rooster" Morrell. Tony founded "Florida's Living History Program," part of his thirty-year quest to connect Floridians with their frontier heritage. *Carlton Ward.*

the backs of Cracker horses, met at the Ayers Ranch and selected the horses that were to be received by the FDACS. That event was well publicized and brought public awareness to what Cracker horses are and just how few of them are left.

During 1985, the Friends of Paynes Prairie Inc. purchased a stallion and five mares from the Ayers Cattle Co. and released them on Paynes Prairie, which had, at one time, been the site of a large Spanish ranch, Rancho de la Chua, the site of the largest Seminole encampment of Natives in North America. The idea was to start a Cracker horse herd there, allowing them to roam free and multiply, as their ancestors did for hundreds of years. Bob Berry of Newberry, Florida, along with Jack Gillen, the manager of Paynes Prairie Preserve State Park, a rancher and a resident of Micanopy, and other ranchers who had Florida Cracker horses and cattle, worked together to accomplish this mission. This event brought more publicity for these Spanish-descended horses and promoted the Cracker horse as a distinct breed.

During the next year, Bob Berry kept his idea of preserving the Cracker horse breed alive by talking with others, including Bobby Hall, who had obtained some of Ayers's horses. Bob's neighbor Buck Mitchell remembered the Cracker horses he rode in his childhood, which led to him obtaining four Cracker mares from Shang Bronson of St. Cloud. By this time, interest was picking up, and they decided it was time to start contacting other Cracker horse people in Florida to set up a meeting. Buck Mitchell and Sam Getzen of Newberry, Jack Gillen of Micanopy, Harvey Ayers of Brooksville and Doug Partin of Kenansville committed to attending a Cracker horse meeting. They contacted other ranchers they knew who might be interested and arranged for a meeting place at the Osceola County Agriculture Center in Kissimmee. Bob Barry placed an advertisement in the November 1988 issue of the *Florida Cattlemen's Magazine*, inviting anyone who owned or was interested in Cracker horses to contact him.

Sixteen people attended the meeting on January 28, 1989, at the Osceola County Center in Kissimmee to consider starting the Cracker Horse Preservation Association: Harvey Ayers of Brooksville; Julie Barry of Fort Lauderdale; Bob Barry, Sam Getzen and Buck Mitchell of Newberry; Elwyn Bass, J.C. Bass, Charles W. Harvey and D.A. Russell of Okeechobee; Jack Gillen of Micanopy; Bobby Hall of San Antonio; Doug Partin and Kevin Whaley of Kenansville; Dave Randall of Lake Wales; and Sergio Bavaqua, originally from South America. Bob Barry presided over the meeting, and Julie served as the secretary. The group favored forming an

Jack Gillen and Ellison Hardee, Paynes Prairie horse herd. *Jane Blais.*

association and seeking assistance from the Florida Division of Agriculture and Consumer Services to get organized and chartered. Subsequent to the meeting, Commissioner Doyle Conner was contacted, and he assured the assistance of his department. The fourteen questionnaires completed at the meeting represented the ownership of ninety Cracker horses. A second organizational meeting in March resulted in the preparation of the first draft of the group's by-laws, which were patterned after those of the Florida Cracker Cattle Breeders Association. The charter of incorporation was granted on April 21, 1989.

The first annual membership meeting was held on June 9, 1989, at Kissimmee. The secretary/treasurer's report showed membership, as of May 30, 1989, comprising ten charter members and ten active members and association funds amounting to $996.30. As noted in the president's report from the first annual membership meeting, the Florida Cracker Horse Association's board served as the evaluation committee to select the foundation horses on which a registry would be based and to set forth criteria for evaluations. The committee operated from the perspective that a breed was being preserved, not created. It was decided that an evaluation team must have three or more qualified members to make valid evaluations. In North Florida, the horses evaluated were either from the Ayers's line or other lines of long standing. In South Florida, most of the horses came from either the Harvey line, which has existed for more than seventy years; the Bronson line; or what might be called the Partin-Whaley line, in which the blood of several Cracker family lines were frequently crossed. "Dan B.," owned by Everett Boals of Gainesville, at the age of thirty, was the oldest horse approved for the foundation's registry. "Dan," who at age twenty-eight had sired three foals from Bob Barry mares, was the last remaining horse of the Thrasher line at Micanopy. The Thrasher horses' line could be traced back to horses caught off Paynes Prairie probably before 1900.

This account would not be complete without giving credit to those cattle ranching families who continued to breed and use Cracker horses over the years, regardless of what others were doing. Without them, we would have no Cracker horses left. So, to the Ayers, Bronsons, Whaleys, Partins, Harveys, Matchetts and others, the Florida Cracker Horse Association says thank you very much. Also, a debt of gratitude is owed to Agriculture Commissioner Doyle Conner, who had the foresight to encourage the preservation of both Cracker horses and Cracker cattle. The assistance of his department and the participation of equine specialist Patti Roberts-Davis were invaluable.

Florida cattlemen continue to breed Cracker horses true to the original breed. Due to the endurance of a few visionary breeders, there is still a nucleus of stock sufficient to assure the preservation of this unique Florida breed. The demand for the Cracker horse continues to increase. The preservation of this unique Florida breed is succeeding, ensuring that this fascinating part of Florida's history will remain alive and well for many generations to come.

The Florida Cracker Horse Association, as a nonprofit corporation, is supported by member volunteers. An eleven-member board, including the president, vice-president and secretary/treasurer, is responsible for the association's day-to-day business and FCHA registry operations. An

"Fancy" (Ayers herd) with Averie, Jennifer and Layna Diapoules. *Author's collection.*

Cowboy polo at a Florida Cracker Horse Association meeting. *Florida Cracker Horse Association Archives.*

annual membership meeting is held each spring for yearly reports, elections and business requiring action from the membership, and Cracker horses are offered for sale at the Florida Cracker Cattle Association's annual Gatherin' and Sale, which allows breeding stock from foundation herds to be shared with all who desire to participate in the preservation efforts. The Florida Department of Agriculture and Consumer Services coordinates and hosts these events, which are held at the Withlacoochee State Forest near Brooksville, Florida. Thanks to the efforts of a group of concerned individuals and Cracker horse owners and the startup assistance from the Florida Department of Agriculture and Consumer Services, a future for the Cracker horse is assured. As of this writing, there are over two thousand horses listed in the Florida Cracker Horse Registry. In her will, benefactor Beverly Zajicek designated that ownership of several of her land holdings be turned over to the Florida Cracker Horse Association to benefit the preservation of the Cracker horse. One such parcel in Bellview, Florida, now know as the Zajicek Preserve, serves as a campground and meeting place for the association.

*The following are stories that serve as testimony to the adaptability, versatility and dependable nature of the Cracker horse.*

## "Flicka": The Oldest Horse in America
### Reprinted from a 1997 newspaper article

Flicka, the 1994 winner of Purina's "Oldest Horse in America" search, will be celebrating his fiftieth birthday in January 1998. He recently was guest of honor at the grand opening of Hunsader's Feed and Mercantile in Bradenton, Florida. He seemed to enjoy all the attention and stood quietly while hundreds of admirers visited with him. Flicka is still in fine health, in spite of some arthritis.

"He leads an easy life now," says owners Sara and Nancy Spanial of Myakka City, Florida. They feed him a special soft diet for older horses, give him plenty of grooming and keep him blanketed on chilly nights in his stall. He is never lonely with his stablemates, an Arab–quarter horse gelding that Nancy has had since he was born twenty-five years ago; and his filly friend, a three-year-old mustang adopted from the Bureau of Land Management. Flicka gets plenty of exercise frolicking and running with them.

Flicka worked as a cow horse for thirty-seven years. When his owner retired, he thought Flicka deserved retirement also, so he gave him to a handicapped riding program, where he took children for rides for seven years. When the program closed, the forty-four-year-old horse was given to Sara Spanial, who was six years old and needed a quiet horse to learn to ride. He has been Sara's companion for six years. When asked what they thought contributed to his longevity, Nancy said:

*I think it's mostly his breeding. He's a Florida Cracker horse, a tough, hardy breed that descends from the early Spanish horses brought to Florida in the 1500s. They grew tough in harsh subtropical climate here and had thick coats to help protect them from insects. For many years, they were the favorite cow ponies of "Cracker cowboys." They've been crossbred for so long, there weren't many left, until recently, when attempts were made to save the breed. Now, there's a registry and stud horses available.*

*Secondly, I guess Flicka's always had good care. In his years as a cow horse, he was worked hard, but he enjoyed working. To this day, he gets excited when we bring the cows in and acts like he wants to help! He was underweight when we got him, but after a few months on good feed, vitamins, pasture and worming, he put on a few hundred pounds and was like a new horse! He has served his purpose well here, as Sara [now twelve] rides horses English, Western, trails and jumping. We love the old horse and will keep taking care of him 'til he dies. We know the day is coming, but for now, he receives the best of care in a well-deserved retirement.*

Happy fiftieth birthday, Flicka!

## "Chiquita"
### By Marjorie Carr

A Florida Cracker horse was my constant companion from 1924 through 1928. I was nine years old when my parents bought Chiquita for me. We lived in an area named Arroyal, located on the Imperial River about three miles west of Bonita Springs, Lee County, Florida. The main object of acquiring Chiquita was to provide me with transportation to and from school, but she was much more than a way to travel to school. With Chiquita, I could visit friends after school, go fishing and swimming in the nearby creeks and

I could go to Bonita Beach, three miles west of Arroyal, to race along the hard, sandy edge of the gulf or go swimming on horseback.

Chiquita, a mare, came from the Kissimmee Prairie, where a large herd of feral horses lived. Cowboys would, from time to time, cut out whatever number of horses they needed. Chiquita had been caught in 1922 and was well trained when my father bought her for me.

My father, a New Hampshire man and a farmer in heritage and at heart, set me up as a horse owner. He built a screened airy barn about eighteen feet square. Mosquitos and horseflies were bad in South Florida. In a corner near the door was a combination tack and feed room. Oats—no corn or sweet feed—were given to Chiquita. My saddle was a modified McClelland (former military) saddle with covered stirrups. I used a straight bit, and Chiquita wore a halter under the bridle all during the day.

A typical school day followed this regimen:

- 6:30 a.m.: Water and feed Chiquita two quarts of oats.
- 7:15 a.m.: Saddle up and ride off to school. A two-quart bag of oats hung on one side of my saddle, my lunch hung on the other. My schoolbooks and a poncho were tied behind.
- 7:45 a.m.: Arrive at the schoolhouse, unsaddle Chiquita and stake her out on an eighteen-foot chain fastened to a two-foot-long bolt hammered into the ground so that she could graze during the morning.
- 12:00 p.m.: Feed and water Chiquita and change her grazing area.
- 3:30 p.m.: Saddle up and either head for home or to some other good location.
- 4:00 p.m.: Brush her down thoroughly and give her water and more oats. If I came early enough, I would stake her out for more grazing. I don't remember ever giving Chiquita hay; grazing and oats were her food. A salt block was always in her feed box.

My ride to school crossed our land, then went up a dirt road, past my aunt and uncle's house, and then went a couple of miles through the pine flat woods to the Bonita Beach dirt road, where it joined the main road from Fort Myers to Naples. The road from Fort Myers to Naples was typical of paved roads in Southwest Florida at that time. The road was made of rolled oyster shells dug from the extensive Indian mounds along the Gulf Coast. Once the roads were washed clean by the rain, they became gleaming white. These shell roads were prone to form wash boards, and periodically, they were scraped to smooth them out.

The oyster shell roads made a good surface for a horse to run on, and if I was tardy, I would let Chiquita out to canter the last half mile to the schoolhouse. Either because I played too long or a rainstorm came up, I sometimes had to make the trip home after dark. I had complete confidence in Chiquita. She trotted right along in the darkening pine woods, dodging the palmettos and gallberries, until she brought me home. Chiquita was a four-gaited horse with an occasional lovely single-foot gait. I never could hold her in the single-foot for any length of time. I wish I had had some knowledge of horse training, for I think she would have been an apt pupil.

There were few people—only two—who had horses for pleasure riding in Bonita Springs. One was an Englishman who had a beautiful Arabian and used an English saddle and, of course, rode English style. The other was a young man named Charlie who was enamored of horses and would have liked to have been a cowboy, but there were no cows in Bonita, only citrus groves. The Englishman came to tea one day, and his beautiful Arabian horse ate our young orange tree. Charlie, who was seven or eight years older than me, rode with me occasionally.

For two years, close family friends and their German shepherd, Blitzen, came to Bonita Springs in the winter. The two boys, near my age, and I played together. Chiquita and Blitzen were always part of our make-believe games— Robin Hood, Indians, circus performers (though we could never stand upright on Chiquita's back) and pioneers. Chiquita was amenable and cooperative and let my two friends ride her without any problem. But at school, she would refuse the attention of the other boys. When I offered to let them try to ride her, she immediately bucked them off! This gave me a certain prestige with my schoolmates, prestige that I needed since I was a Yankee, a girl and wore pants to school. I wore whip cord riding pants with high socks. (I always wanted boots, but my feet grew too fast to warrant the cost of boots.)

The Bonita school went through only the eighth grade, so when I reached the ninth, we had to move to Fort Myers. We found a good family with children for Chiquita, and I think she led a happy life with them.

—Marjorie Harris Carr, October 28, 1996

*Marjorie formed a group to stop the digging of a cross-Florida barge canal, which would have destroyed the flow of the Ocklawaha and Silver Rivers. A land bridge that crosses Interstate 75 now bears her name and adjoins the Florida Cracker Horse Association property near Belview, Florida; article courtesy of Florida Cracker Horse Association Archives.*

## *"Dollie"*
### *By Iris Wall*

In the early 1940s, Indiantown was a great place to grow up. Talk about "born free"—that was us, cow hunting, fishing, swimming, anything that crossed our minds. My family ran our cattle with a group of men that included Ralph Hamrick, Uncle Quinn Bass and his sons Archie, Eddie and Elmer on land owned by the Southern States Land Timber Company all the way from Indiantown to Palm City. Those men were so kind and respectful to my sister June and me.

My horse was named Dollie. She was a little blue roan Cracker mare about fourteen and a half hands high. I've never seen a horse like her before or since. June and I would ride our horses to school and anchor them out during school. Gerald Matthews said the whole school would line up when school was out to see if we'd get bucked off. We were usually riding something half wild. Our father was a sort of horse trader. He'd go to Tampa and bring home a truckload at a time, and he'd say, "Go to 'em, gals." And that's exactly what we did. Can you imagine allowing kids to do that today? The world is so different.

Every Sunday afternoon, we all got together for some horse racing. Sometimes, we had the races in Indiantown, and sometimes, we had them in Palm City. All the men would stand around and brag about their horses. My sister June and I weighed less than one hundred pounds, so folks always wanted us to ride their horses for them. Some of the old timers who came were Clady Savage, Noah Ludlum, Sandy McKenzie, Toots Morgan, Archie Bass and many more. Dollie could outrun any horse there for 150 yards. She just loved to run. We rode with only a bridle, and I loved to ride her. Believe me, we made a good pair.

I've seen my father rope thirty-five calves in one day and doctor them for screwworms. We would ride every day we weren't in school, and I've never seen Dollie tired. You never needed any spurs. She would run at the touch of a heel to her sides or simply lowering the reins to allow her some room. Myrle Williams bought some angus cattle, and we had a Brahma bull, so we produced some Brangus calves that were big and mean. Once, we were working some cattle, and a great, big yearling jumped out. Dad jumped on Dollie with an old saddle to rope the yearling. Just as Dollie jumped the ditch, the cow hit the end of the rope and jerked the saddle to Dollie's side, causing my father to fall and break several ribs. It was a sight to behold to see Dollie, with that saddle on her side, keep that yearling off Daddy until we could get him out of reach.

*Opposite, top*: "Fancy" (Ayers herd) getting relief from the South Florida heat with Easton Storey. *Author's collection.*

*Opposite, bottom*: Sawyer and Toni Beyer with "Huckleberry" (Bronson/Mitchell herds). *Author's collection.*

*Left*: Eva Vergara's first ride on "Cazadora de la Vaca," Hunter of the Cow, (Ayers/Bronson/Mitchell herds). *Author's collection.*

Ava Redding on "Felicia" (Ayers/Bronson/Mitchell herds) with Tamara Redding and Haley Naramore. *Author's collection.*

Ben Feely's groomsmen riding Cracker horses and a Cracker mule. *Shelby and Ben Feely, wedding photograph.*

*Above*: Waylon Mitchell riding "Monte" (Ayers/Bronson/Harvey herds) GFCD 2022. *Author's collection.*

*Left*: Circle boss Cracker Jack Gillen and his wife, "Mama Jack," GFCD 2022. *Author's collection.*

After my husband, Homer, and I married, we took her to Immokalee, and she died there while giving birth to a colt. In those days, you never thought of getting a vet, and we were camped too far out to get one anyway. I've never had a horse as good as she, and I've never had one I loved more.

## *Florida Cracker Cattle: Florida's Heritage Cattle*

*A Cracker cow can hide a calf where a Philadelphia lawyer couldn't find it until she's ready to come back and get it!*
—*Iris Wall*

Cattle were independently domesticated from the aurochs, a wild bovine species that were one and a half to two times the size of present-day domestic cattle and roamed in the vicinity of the current countries of Turkey and Pakistan ten thousand years ago. Cattle have since spread across the world. The word *cattle* does not have a singular form, aside from the technical term *head of cattle*. There isn't a single word that means specifically a single head of cattle of unstated gender and age. As such, even though it's technically inaccurate, *cow* is generally used in informal situations as the singular form of *cattle*.

Today's Florida breed of heritage cattle, the Florida Cracker cattle, are descended from the original cattle brought by the Spanish in the 1500s. In 2007, in St. Augustine, archaeologist Carl Halbirt conducted an excavation of an abandoned Spanish colonial water well site. Among the artifacts found were broken pottery, metal objects and glass fragments, along with skeletal cattle remains from a Spanish cow that were dated to around 1600. In 2012, local rancher Allan Roberts from First Coast Cattle LLC conducted a DNA analysis comparing the DNA from blood samples of his Florida Cracker cattle to DNA from cows' teeth found in the skeletal remains of the well. The results of the DNA analysis confirmed the Cracker cattle from the Roberts herd were closely related to the four-hundred-plus-year-old cow whose teeth were found in the well.

Today's Florida Cracker cattle vary from the very small (these animals are often referred as guinea cattle), weighing no more than 500 pounds at maturity, to cows comparable to "average-sized" commercial beef cows (that is, weighing from 950 to 1,000 pounds). These larger Florida Cracker cattle are more likely to be seen in cattle that were selected for larger breed size and a more "beef-type" conformation than those in the more northern areas of our state. These cattle might also descend from those that were referred to as the piney woods cattle of Georgia, Alabama and Mississippi. One such herd of these cattle was maintained for many years by the Barnes family of Florala, Alabama, just across the border from Northwest Florida. Cracker cattle are hardy, disease and pest resistant and forage during the winter when other breeds require feed. Cracker cows live longer, producing more calves continually throughout the years—every nine months and often until the last year of their lives.

The coloration and spotting patterns of Florida Cracker cattle are quite varied and resemble those of the Texas longhorn. It is likely that the majority of the Florida Cracker cattle of yesteryear were solid red, solid black or solid brown mixed with a few brindles. There would have been some spotted animals, some linebacks (somewhat similar to the Pinzgauer cattle) and a few spotted (like Holsteins or Guernseys), maybe the descendants of crosses between Cracker bulls and the family milk cows the early colonists brought with them from Georgia and the Carolinas. Another spotting pattern that would have been prevalent in the past and still exists today is called color-sided by geneticists but might be more commonly recognized by the name frosty linebacks. Animals with this type of coloring can be differentiated by their sprinkling of white, roaning or dappling on their faces, which is absent on cattle with the previously named type of lineback spotting pattern. Animals with extensive speckles and spots, as well as roan and nearly white animals (usually with pigmented ears) are sometimes seen and are acceptable colorations.

The general low level of nutrition available on range lands and unfertilized pastures, along with the rough woods—the scrub, as it is called in Florida— where these cattle spent most of their time, likely affected the size of the Florida Cracker cattle and their horns. The horns of Florida Cracker cattle have a greater tendency to go up rather than out like those of their relatives the Texas longhorns. This tendency to go up was often observed in photographs of Florida Cracker cattle from the 1930s and prior. This adaptation likely benefited the cattle as they ran through the scrub, since the brush and low-lying trees would have made it difficult for animals with wider

Brindle-colored Cracker bull "Sweet Pea" owned by Aaron and Laura Gavronsky. *Author's collection.*

*Top*: A brown cow/ calf pair. *Dr. Tim Olsen.*.

*Middle*: A brown cow/ black calf pair. *Dr. Tim Olsen.*

*Bottom*: A blue roan cow/black calf pair. *Dr. Tim Olsen.*

*Top*: A red and white lineback with speckling pair. *Dr. Tim Olsen.*

*Middle*: A black, brown, white with speckling cow/tan brindled lineback with a speckling calf pair. *Dr. Tim Olsen.*

*Bottom*: A black, brown and white lineback cow/red and black brindle with a white lineback calf pair. *Dr. Tim Olsen.*

horns to maneuver. Some of the horns of the oldest Cracker cows that are the most distinctive of the breed rise up quickly without going out far and then turn back at their ends in a sort of lyre fashion. The horns of Florida Cracker cattle should not be wide at their bases, as this is indicative of "outside" breeding—Brahman influence in particular.

*The following is from the address for the 1995 Cracker Cattle Symposium, which was given by Florida's commissioner of agriculture Doyle Conner Sr.*

*The year of the Florida sesquicentennial celebration is an appropriate time for us to reflect back on our rich heritage. I am the fifth generation in my family to own Florida Cracker Cattle. These cattle were identified by different names by different people. Reference was made to pine woods cows, scrub cows, native cattle, and, yes, Cracker cows. It is a well-known fact that the Cracker cow put Florida in the cattle business. The hardy little Cracker cow crossed well with bulls of any breed. Cross we did until hardly a pure Cracker cow could be found in Florida.*

*Everyone agrees we successfully crossed for better beef, but we were breeding away from the native Cracker cow. For ages, the Cracker cow never changed. In the 1930s and 1940s, most Florida ranches began using Angus, Hereford, Shorthorn and Brahman bulls. Many ranches, particularly in South Florida, developed Brahman influence in their cattle. Our family had unimproved Cracker cattle until after World War II. All of our bulls were selected from the Cracker herd. I remember a blue guinea bull my father valued highly. He did have a long body but no other desirable qualities. My dad liked him because he stayed fat all year.*

*When I was in high school, our family had Cracker cattle on the open range. Screwworms infested Florida in those days, and all men in the family rode every day, doctoring those pesky little critters. The competition was keen between my two brothers, Glenn and Lucian, and me to determine who doctored the most cases of screwworms on a given day. Our mother constantly reprimanded us for discussing this subject at the supper table.*

*I was pleased to be in the legislature in the 1950s and help pass the Screwworm Eradication Bill. The eradication of the screwworm in the United States will always be an important benchmark in the advancement of the cattle industry in our country. Now, I would like to mention the events leading up to the preservation of the Cracker cow and Cracker horses. As time moved on, I suddenly realized that the Cracker animals were rapidly vanishing. Because of my interest in pioneer Florida, I realized we could not simply stand by and watch these animals disappear from our environment. I called the president of the Florida Cattlemen's Association and asked him to help locate some typical Florida Cracker cattle.*

*The Bass family of Okeechobee received the assignment, perhaps because they still owned some of the James Durrance's strain of Cracker cows. J.C. Bass led the effort of putting the first group [of] cattle together. J.C. made available four heifers and one bull to the Department of Agriculture. The herd was maintained on the Department of Agriculture's property in the early days. Later, as the herd grew in size, a second herd was established in the Withlacoochee State Forest. The Florida Park Service obtained cattle from Zeb Durrance [James's son] and from the Chaires family of Dixie County to start the herd at Lake Kississimee State Park and Paynes Prairies Preserve State Park. Some cattle from the John and Woody Tilton family of Palatka also were added to the Paynes Prairie herd. The herd, now located in the Withlacoochee State Forest, was formed from the surplus produced in the Department of Agriculture's herd in Tallahassee, along with some extra animals from Paynes Prairie. These herds have been selected over the years to maintain the historical size, coloration and spotting and horn shapes of the cattle of the 1800s. Pictures of Florida Cracker cattle from as early as 1908 are in existence; they provided useful guides during the selection process. Specifically, we eliminated cattle with traits of Brahman, Hereford and other modern-day cattle breeds, sometimes through the use of blood typing. I passed the word that if anyone was caught improving these cattle with modern bulls, it would be wise to seek other employment. For thirty years, the Cracker cow quietly made her way back into Florida history.*

*Today, the Department of Agriculture owns about sixty head of the prime Cracker cattle. These animals have gone through a DNA screening process to establish their ancestry. Animals with the slightest amount of modern bloodlines were promptly eliminated from the herd. After thirty years of rebuilding their numbers, it is time for the Cracker cow to take center stage on the Florida and Southeastern cattle scene.*

*I recommended that we form a Cracker Cattle Breeders Association here in Florida. The first meeting was held in Tallahassee. Cracker cattle owners from Mississippi, Alabama, Georgia and all parts of Florida showed up for the meeting. There was no doubt the organization was destined to be a huge success. The Cracker Cattle Breeders Association was formed to preserve the breed, not for economic gain or any sort of better beef type program. My vision was to see old timers lead typical Cracker cattle through the livestock arena at the Florida State Fair in Tampa, not for competition but to show where we were in the early days and where we are today.*

*Beginning in 1988, annual Florida Cracker Cattle Association meetings are held at the Withlacoochee State Forest. During the annual meeting, an auction sale of Cracker cattle and Cracker horses is held. Individual breeders, as well as the Department of Agriculture, offer animals to the general public at this auction. The Cracker cattle will now forever be preserved as living links to Florida's past. After being rediscovered, it has now been recognized and listed as one of five outstanding rare breeds in North America.*

*Florida Cracker cow hunters are known to tell colorful cow hunting stories around the campfire at night. The following is a story from the time Paynes Prairie was a working cattle ranch called Camp Ranch.*

## *"O.D. Catches the Train"*
## *By Butch Hunt*

O.D. came to us with the longest lariat I'd ever seen tied to a saddle that looked as if it'd be drug from Punta Gorda to Georgia. That rope must have been sixty feet long. He'd worked for Lykes Brothers last on those sawgrass prairies south of here, down Fish-Eating Creek way. If you've ever been down there along Highway 441, you know there are places where, outside of an occasional cabbage palm island, there are thousands of acres of nothing. There's just that—nothing, except north toward Lake Okeechobee (a high dike now) and the Cow Creek Reservation.

Now, Florida cowboys were never that—they were cow hunters, so called from earliest times, perhaps because unlike the West, with its unending plains and limitless vistas, Florida is as apt to be jungle or hammock as wetland prairie. You spend a lot of time just hunting cattle here, and of course, it only starts with the finding. These used to be woods-wise cattle that could fade away like the deer that shared their grazing in hidden glades and pocket prairies.

The sixty-foot rope was a necessity if you'd worked for Lykes back then; you packed enough grub for a week when you left headquarters on your pony, knowing you might not see a man for days. There might come times when you'd be glad of that rope's length when you tied onto a cow fighting for her calf, half eaten by screwworms. You couldn't pass one up in those days. Every newborn calf seemed to have it. The barest hint of blood, and the fly laid its eggs that hatched soon enough to eat an animal alive if a ranch hand didn't come along to treat it.

Common sense dictated that you tote more than one rope. One for the calf, and one for the cow who spent her time really wanting to "eat your lunch" while you dug those worms out of her calf and squirted that nasty black stuff into the wound.

You have to remember that you'd be alone—except for your pony, of course—and trees were a scarce commodity. When you got done treating the calf and loosed it, there was Mamma, mad and mean on the end of a rope.

Now, there are a lot of ways to get a rope off a cow that has horns and wants nothing more than to stick one through your liver and lights. However, every way has its drawbacks and hinges on something between skill and luck in equal parts.

The sixty-foot rope is only an edge in that situation. First of all, you have to realize that for a Florida cow hunter to lose his rope is not only a financial disaster but a social taboo of long standing. Many a cow hunter never came back rather than come back without his rope. Unlike some western cowboys, Florida men tie hard and fast to the saddle horn—no dallys, and until death us do part. Like many ill-planned marriages, this one can have dire consequences for all concerned.

Seems he'd been out about four days, had doctored a slew of calves and had eaten most of his grub (and what salt pork he had left was getting pretty rank). He had a couple of cans of beans and a little coffee left in his sack, and that was about it. Pretty soon, he'd have to turn north, head toward the creek and met up again or make the even longer ride back to headquarters to draw some pay and kill a day or two in Immokolee.

He didn't want to leave the area yet. There was an old cow with twisty horns, and she had a new calf. He'd seen her a couple of times, but she was slick and seldom got far from Church House Hammock. She'd come out on the prairie now and then but usually only early or late, when the deer flies got too bad in the trees. The calf was a week old, its navel infested with screwworm. No one but he would ever know if he bypassed that one calf, but he'd know. You take a man's money to do a job, and he takes your word you'll do it, and that's enough. It's been enough for centuries and means more to a certain breed of man than all the money in the First National Bank and all the fame and pride of being president of these United States. There will always be men like that, God willing. Not all of them are cowmen.

O.D. had an idea where that cow was and how to get her. He'd lost her last time because she'd dove in a thicket just as he'd flung his rope. The old

Seaboard Railway had a line that bisected that hammock, and a train came through there once a day, just before dark that time of year. Wood cows are like deer in that they can hear you coming a half mile away and smell you, too, if the wind is right. O.D. had been hunting cows long enough to know their habits, and after losing this one a couple of times, he'd spent some time quartering the hammock until he learned her trails, where she watered and where she bedded down. Most often, she was close to the tracks when night came. He determined to be close himself this last afternoon. He figured the noise from the train's passage would enable him to get near enough to get his rope on the cow, snub her to a tree and then catch the calf. Then he could go to Immokolee and do what any fella his age with thirty or forty dollars in his pocket could do in town. He felt that the possibility for committing nuisance were limitless.

He tied his horse two hundred yards from the tracks, even though the wind was in his favor, and crept the remaining distance to the area that all his cow sense told him old twist-horn called hers. Sure enough, he hadn't settled in good before he heard the calf bawl and felt rather than heard the low grunt of the cow's reply. He wanted a cigarette badly but put it out of his mind. The cow would certainly smell it if the wind quartered. In ten minutes, he was rewarded by a flicker of movement on the far side of the railway embankment. It was the calf, tormented by flies, its tail whipping. It bawled again.

The sun was low. O.D. didn't own a watch, but with the certainty of a man who spent his days under sun and stars, he knew it was close to time for the train. He eased out of his hidey hole and made his way back to his horse. He tightened the saddle girth, looked to that sixty-foot rope and felt his right pocket. All cowmen carry a knife of some sort, usually a pocketknife that is kept razor sharp for a variety of reasons. Often, it's needed to perform field operations on livestock. If small horn buds are excised carefully, that calf will never have horns in maturity. Every cattle owner has a registered brand and a registered earmark as well. Those earmarks are made with a pocketknife, sometimes long before the general roundup, during which the animal will be branded properly. Often, the knife is used to castrate bull calves. In plain fact, that same sharp knife can and has saved many a cowman's life. The tales are apocryphal perhaps—the cutting of the stirrup leather after being dragged for miles or freedom from an entanglement of horse, rider and cow that would certainly have ended in death to the man otherwise. Whatever the reason—if for no other than the fact that O.D. frequented bars on his rare trips to town seemed to warrant it—he kept his knife sharp, and he kept it close.

O.D. heard the train coming. It was still a mile or two away. He mounted up and eased the piece of split leather that secured the long lariat off his saddle horn. He shook out a loop and transferred the bulk of the rope's length to his left hand. As the train came closer, he kneed the horse forward. All depended on timing now. Cow and calf were on the far side of the tracks. Too soon, and the cow would see or hear him and be off into a darkening thicket with the calf. Gauging the train's approach, he rode faster, hoping to catch a glimpse of the intended prey just before the locomotive eclipsed his view. With luck, the cow wouldn't see him, and as the last car passed, he'd be over the embankment and on her before she knew it. As the engine roared into view, he made his approach. His timing was off! The cow sensed or heard him. A split second before the locomotive passed between them, the cow raised her head and saw horse and rider headed her way. Up came her tail, and O.D. had time to realize that she was running, on the other side, going flat out racing the train. Then giving one moment to eye the length of the train, O.D. found himself in a dead run on his side, heading in the same direction. His only thought was to be in the same place when the train passed. After the engine and a couple of cars had roared by, O.D. caught a fleeting glimpse of the cow through the gap between a couple of freight cars and could see that she was still on course, hugging the railway embankment, as if trying to outrun the train. Who knows what goes through a cow's mind at the best of times? O.D. figured either she was using the train as a blind, the same way he'd tried, or she was making a dash for open prairie and alongside the tracks was the quickest and most open ground for her to get there. He found that he couldn't center all of his attention on the gaps between cars, because the terrain demanded he keep an eye out for obstacles as well. The myrtle thickets along the right-of-way were patchy but unpredictable. Some grew close enough to the tracks to force him to detour to the outside. As he risked a look back, a limb took his hat. His horse leaped a discarded crosstie. Horse and cow couldn't keep this up much longer. Seemed as though they'd already come a mile and wide open all the way. There were only a half-dozen cars left to pass.

He caught another glimpse of the cow as a float car overtook him. She was only a couple of lengths ahead, head low and stretched out for all she was worth. The calf had probably been left far behind, but no matter; he'd attend to the cow and go back for the calf. His horse's labored breathing was audible even over the noise of the wheels on rail, the *clickety clack* and poppin' of ballast stone. He saw the cow again, and for a moment, they were neck and neck at the gap between the last car and the caboose. Slobber streamed from her open mouth, and from the glazed look in her eye, he knew she'd run until she dropped.

In another moment, he saw the startled face of a brakeman at a window, and O.D. was whirling his loop, the horse heaving, clawing obliquely up the left side of the embankment as the tail end of the caboose drew near. Now, O.D. told me that parts of what happened next have never been to clear to him since. Having luck take some bizarre turns once or twice, I can well understand.

As the end of the caboose swept by his right shoulder, he could see that the cow had cut to her right and as the railroad emptied out onto flat prairie, she'd be so far ahead in two more jumps that he'd never catch her on a played-out horse. All in a split second, two things occurred which, although they didn't spoil his aim, must have affected his judgement. The rear door of the caboose was opened by the brakeman, who lunged into view, his mouth wide in query. O.D.'s horse stumbled as he flung the rope. In the seconds that followed, O.D. was unaware that his loop settled perfectly over the twisty horns of that old cow. His horse had indeed buckled at the knees and started a forward somersault down the embankment.

O.D. said that he only had a second to think, and all he could think of was that he'd probably end up under those caboose wheels, and that dang cow would get clean away. In the next second, horse and rider were arrested in their fall with a jerk and surge upward. The rope had tightened in time to help. His horse, however, seemed unable to stop moving forward. His front legs were braced, feet scotching, sending up showers of ballast rock as he proceeded down the track in a series of jolting hops and frantic leaps. To his horror, O.D. realized that somehow, he'd either thrown his rope on the wrong side of the back porch guardrail, or through it or something. At any rate, horse, rider and cow were hitched to the ass-end of a Seaboard freight train that was picking up speed now that it had gained the long straightaway out on the flats.

O.D. said that it all happened quicker than he could ever tell it. He saw that the cow had been thrown when the rope tightened up. In fact, she had done a back flip high enough for the brakeman to see daylight under her. Now, it was a good-sized cow, and O.D. was on one of those small Cracker ponies, but the pony was on his feet (more or less), and the cow was sliding along on the keel of her backbone, so pretty soon, the cow fetched up at the edge of the caboose at the guardrail. Well, O.D. said that even a fella with no more schoolin' than him could see what was happening next, and he was trying to claw that pocketknife out to cut the rope and never you mind what anybody thought about it. Sure enough, when the cow bottomed out on the railing, the pony took off like a big bird, and when they hit the rocks, O.D. dropped the knife to hold on.

I asked him why he hadn't already bailed off that horse before things got that serious. He just looked at me awhile and said that although he'd been thrown many a time, he had never let it happen on purpose, and besides, it hadn't occurred to him. Why, to go back without a rope would be bad enough, but how to explain a rope, a saddle and a horse—not to mention that dang crooked horn cow?

Anyway, as soon as the horse hit the ground, the weight of the cow began to tell, and soon, horse, rider and cow were paralleling one another, still on opposite sides of the tracks. O.D. said it was dreadful the way that cow bellowed, with half her hair worn off her and getting worse with every yard down the track. Him and the horse weren't doing much better, and the only good thing was his leg wasn't trapped underneath, but the bad thing was, the other foot was through the stirrup, and he was married to that saddle, like it or not. He had one hand on the rope, hoping the horn would pull right out of the saddle and grappling with his boot and the stirrup, but the way those railroad ties had them porpoising up and down, it was about all he could do to hang on. They were gaining on the train, thanks to the heavier cow.

The brakeman was hangin' over the railing, but O.D. couldn't tell what the guy was yelling. If he hadn't dropped his knife—"Cut the rope!" O.D. yelled.

"Whaaat?" yelled the brakeman.

"Cut the dang rope!" screamed O.D.

"Caaan't heeear you!" yelled the brakeman.

O.D. was desperate. He didn't think either he or his pony would live long enough to be pulled to the railing. And if they were, then what? He found the girth strap with his fingers and fumbled, one handed, at the knot. The saddle was already pulled over the pony's withers, forcing his front legs forward, pressing the neck down. Suddenly the saddle slipped free! O.D. said it addled him some when he fetched up against that guardrail and likely he'd of been jerked clean on around it and off the other side (at least most of him), but somehow or other, that idiot brakeman got in the way and got all tangled up in the rigging of the saddle, and there they both were, hanging on the rail for dear life, screaming away with a half ton of cow trying to pull them off into a twilight prairie.

Suddenly, the wrenching pressure was gone! O.D. levered himself up painfully on an elbow and looked back into the gathering dusk. Several hundred yards down the track stood his pony, head down. As he watched, the cow, much closer, gained her feet. There was enough light to see that old twisty horn had only one horn left. Suddenly, in silhouette, he saw twisty-horn trot across the tracks, toward the pony, shaking her head in rage. The pony fled, apparently on four good legs.

O.D. gathered up his lariat, its now empty end knotted and trailing. "Shoot!" exclaimed the brakeman in undisguised awe.

"Where's this train stop?" asked O.D.

"Don't stop till Jacksonville," was the reply.

"@*#^!" said O.D. The whistle blew, and the train rattled on into the night.

Well, they found O.D.'s horse eventually, but it wasn't until months later that any of the Lykes Brothers' hands found out what had happened to O.D. Cowhands move around some, and they're always drifting from one job to another. O.D. was at the Ocala Stock Market one day and found one of those fellas he'd known down there staring at him.

"O.D! We thought you was dead!"

"Naw, I ain't." he replied. The fella shook his head.

"Your pony showed up one day lookin' like he'd been clawed by bears and all the hair wore off one side. We looked some, whenever we had a chance—but never found a sign of you except a hat and a pocketknife down there near those myrtle thickets by the tracks."

"See anything of an old one-horn cow and her calf?"

"Yeah. We found her. Looked worse than your horse—four hairs on one side and three on the other. She was so stove up, she was easy to catch. Probably freeze to death this winter. Slick as a monkey's butt all over." The cowhand grinned.

"Serves her right," O.D. nodded.

"What happened to you? It was mighty mysterious. Figured if the train had run over you, there'd be parts left on the tracks; more sign than we found."

"I reckon you can say I caught the train. I don't even want to talk about it," said O.D.

The cowhand shook his head in bewilderment and left. In such ways, legends are born. In a year or two, there were hands ready to swear that they'd been riding with O.D. when he took the notion to spur his horse up and swing up on a freight car headed north. Hairless horses or cows only tend to complicate an admiring tale told by firelight. There wasn't a one of them hadn't at some time or other wanted to ride a lonesome whistle out of there.

## Tools of the Trade

### *Florida Cow Dogs*

*Three cattlemen were overheard bragging about driving cattle. The first was from Montana and made this declaration, "A good Montana cow crew can drive one thousand head of cattle a thousand miles with only five cowboys." To which the Texas cattleman replied, "Shoot! A Texas cow crew can drive one thousand head of cattle a thousand miles with three cowboys!" Leaning back in his chair, the Florida cowman looked at the other men and stated, "A Florida cowboy can do it all by himself with four dogs—and faster! Game on, boys!"*
—*from a conversation between "Mr. Montana" and the author*

In 1770, naturalist William Bartram observed a single dog, trained by the Seminoles to work stock, keep a group of horses under control. "A troop of horses under the control of a single black dog, which seemed to differ in no respect from the wolf of Florida, except his being able to bark as the common dog. He was very careful and industrious in keeping them together, and if anyone strolled from the rest at too great a distance, the dog would spring up, head the horse and bring him back to the company." The origins of Florida cow dogs and cow dog work practices are not easily traced. There were early Spanish influences. De Soto, for example, brought stock dogs to Florida in 1539. British and Celtic cultures have long histories of using dogs to herd cattle and sheep, and many of the ancestors of Florida cattle-ranching families were people of British and Celtic origin from Georgia and the Carolinas who settled in frontier Florida in the eighteenth and nineteenth centuries. Native peoples also used dogs as work animals.

After the Civil War, dogs served in important roles in the process of gathering up the wild cattle and shipping them to Cuba. Dogs helped the cow hunters with the difficult and dangerous task of flushing wild cattle from the scrub and swamps. They then helped keep herds together as they drove them to holding pens at Tampa, Fort Myers and Punta Rassa on the southern coast of the Gulf of Mexico.

When artist Frederic Remington visited Florida in the late nineteenth century to document cowmen, he found a rough and ragged lot who, in his opinion, did not compare with the dashing, romanticized cowboys of the West. In an article published in the August 1895 issue of *Harper's New Monthly Magazine*, Remington wrote, "But they are picturesque in their unkept, almost unearthly wildness. A strange effect is added by their use of large, fierce cur dogs, one of which accompanies each cattle hunter and is taught to pursue the cattle and even take them by the nose. Still, as they have only a couple horses apiece, it saves them much extra running."

Florida cow dogs are bred with one purpose in mind: to produce dogs that work well with cattle. Specific breeds might work well in the mix. Probably the most popular is the southern black-mouth yellow cur, also known simply as the blackmouth cur. Although its origins are debated, it is now a recognized and registered breed. Another breed popular today is the Catahoula leopard dog, which has its origins among the French or Natives of Lousiana, depending on which claims one chooses to believe. But the Florida cowman has no interest in purebred dogs—they are usually too nervous or have other weaknesses. Good cow dogs might contain strains of cur for all-around endurance and good working traits; hound for long wind; and bulldog for strength and aggressiveness. Mature male dogs usually weigh between sixty and seventy pounds, and females weigh five to ten pounds less.

Okeechobee ranch foreman and third-generation cattleman Keith Bass described the varieties of Florida cow dogs he has encountered: "They just got a kind of a little round lookin' head on 'em, kind of short-eared. Not like a bulldog. Kind of got short hair on 'em. Some of 'em is stub-tailed. Some of 'em is long-tailed. Some of 'em is yellow lookin' dogs with a black mouth. I've seen some brindle dogs, leopard, too."

Florida cowmen overwhelmingly prefer dogs from bloodlines known to produce good cow dogs. For example, a cowman might proudly announce that his dogs are descended from those bred by the Partins of Osceola County, a family that has produced top-notch cow dogs for at least one hundred years.

To maintain a quality line of dogs, breeders are always looking for another good line with which to crossbreed theirs. Lines for crossbreeding are selected strictly by reputation for producing excellent work dogs, and such arrangements are often made between old friends.

Florida cow dogs perform three principal functions. First, they flush strays from hammocks, scrubs and swamps, easily working in areas that are very difficult if not impossible to penetrate by horse and rider. George "Junior" Mills of Okeechobee worked cattle throughout Central Florida for more than seven decades. He considered cow dogs invaluable. "Them dogs is just as important, in a way, as a horse is. He can get in places you can't get, you know. I went one time to gather a bunch of cattle on the old Uncle Wright Carlton place. Them cattle down there, you couldn't handle 'em. You couldn't hardly do nothin' with 'em without dogs. They'd run in them hammocks and hide. You put them dogs in there, and them dogs make it so hot for 'em, they got to get outa there."

The dogs also control the movement of the cattle. As the mounted cowmen patiently drive the cattle forward from the rear, the dogs work on the sides and in front to keep the stock in a cohesive herd. The dogs do not drive the cattle. Because Florida cow dogs approach the heads of cattle to control their movement, they are known as "headers."

The third function the dogs perform is to hold the cattle in a tight bunch once the stock arrives at a particular destination. The dogs accomplish this by repeatedly circling or "ringing" the cattle, all while barking, nipping at the cattle and generally giving them a hard time.

The dogs are bred for this work and no doubt enjoy it. Often, it all seems a big game as they frolic and romp. Many owners say the only training they have to give the dogs is to teach them to come back. The dogs instinctively know how to fetch strays and keep a herd tightly bunched. Starting with inherited knowledge and behavior, younger dogs learn the finer points from working with the older dogs. Cowmen speak of "dog-broke" cattle. Cattle that have never been worked by dogs do not respond well to them. Cattle that are used to working with dogs, or cattle that are "dog-broke," respond quickly to the physical messages and sonic cues dogs give them. Because a rancher never sells their entire herd, there is always some fraction of the herd accustomed to working with dogs, thus the working relationship between cattle and dogs is perpetuated.

Reminiscing about nearly seven decades of riding Florida range, Junior Mills told a story that illustrates how tough the dogs can be. While working in Marion County in 1949, his horse fell into a sinkhole that had already swallowed a dog and a cow. His workmate rode into Ocala and returned about two hours later with a wrecker to winch the horse from the hole. As they freed the steaming, exhausted horse, it took one last breath and died. The cow's back was broken by the weight of the horse and had to be shot. Only the dog survived, and it had been at the bottom of the pile. Mills fished a rope down to the feisty canine. "He just reached out and bit it and shut down on the rope," he recalled. Mills and his partner hauled the dog out of the hole by the strength of its jaw. After resting a good while in the shade of a cabbage palm, the dog was ready for more.

Most Florida cowmen agree that a cow dog is mighty handy. Saddle-maker and ranch hand Mike Wilder from Keenansville expressed an opinion shared by many Florida cowmen: "When you really need 'em, one good dog is worth three or four men." Billy Davis, a highly skilled

Jack Gillen with "Dazzle" (Ayers herd) and Florida cur dog "Janie." *Bob Stone.*

Osceola County cowman, quipped, "Now, I don't know if I'm just sorry help, or I've just got good dogs, but a dog is just the handiest thing in the world around a bunch of cattle."

*This account was documented and shared with permission from Bob Stone, outreach coordinator for the Florida Folklife Program, division of Historical Resources, Florida Department of State, www.flheritage.com/preservation.*

*The following articles have appeared in monthly editions of the* Florida Cattleman and Livestock Journal, *written by Bob Stone, and were shared with permission from the Florida Cattlemen's commissioned by the Florida Cattlemen's Foundation in its mission to preserve the history and culture of the Florida beef cattle industry.*

## Saddles
### Mike Wilder

When he was eleven years old, seventh-generation Floridian Mike Wilder spent the summer helping his paternal grandfather gather and work cattle on his Hillsborough County ranch. "Of course, back then, all the cattle were caught by hand. I worked the whole summer for fifty dollars. Having this much fun and getting paid was a major factor in choosing to be a cowboy. I loved the cowboy life!" recalled the burly, soft-spoken craftsman.

Mike's ancestors moved from Georgia to settle in the Knight's Station community, near present-day Plant City, in the 1840s. Mike was born in

1954 in Tampa to Yvonne and Keith Wilder. Tragically, his father drowned when Mike was about a year and a half old; his mother never remarried, and Mike is an only child. Mike does not have much detailed information about his ancestors but does recall his mother saying that her mother had immigrated to Tampa from Sicily and worked in the cigar factories in Ybor City.

About two weeks before graduating from Brandon High School in 1972, Mike and his buddy Matt Hopper heard they were hiring cowboys at Junior Padgett's Turkey Hammock Ranch, a huge spread that stretched from the east side of Lake Kissimmee to Kenansville and south of State Road 60. They traveled to the ranch and were hired. "I graduated on Tuesday and left for the job at 4:00 a.m. Wednesday," Mike recalled. "I was eighteen, and I think the oldest man on the crew was twenty or twenty-one. There were six or seven of us at any given time. We lived in a bunkhouse and had a cook." The days were long, and the pay was short. "We usually worked five and a half days a week, and I started off at sixty dollars a week. Sometimes, in a good week, I made a dollar an hour. Most of the time, it was a little less. Things were a lot more manual then," he recalled. "We had a squeeze chute, but there was no calf table. We still dipped cattle in vats and sprayed them, too."

Mike continued, "Because of my size, I was one of the muggers." In those days blood was drawn from the necks of cattle. "Every cow that came in, we had to catch their head, pull their head over and hold it while a vet drew their blood. Back then, most of the cattle had horns, which, in a way, made it easier. Of course, you had to dodge 'em." Mike recalled there being about three thousand to four thousand cattle at Turkey Hammock in those days.

After Mike saw an advertisement in *Western Horseman* magazine for a saddle-making school in Whitewood, South Dakota, he enrolled in the program at J.M. Saddlery, where he studied from October 1976 through May 1977, the coldest months of the year during a particularly cold winter. "I damn near froze to death up there!" he declared. Upon his return from South Dakota, Mike worked for Deseret Ranch for about a year and a half, and then he worked for Fellsmere Farms.

Mike finally settled down in 1981, when he married Brenda Anastasio. Brenda and Mike have two daughters, Bridget (Coggins) and Stacey (Handley). Toward the end of his tenure at Lokosee Ranch, he purchased land just north of Kenansville, on which his family built a home and shop. "This was nothing but a palmetto patch," he recalled. "I borrowed a tractor and thoroughly disked the land." The family worked as a team to clear the land. "My wife, the girls and I all worked together. It was well worth the effort to have our own place."

While employed at various ranches, Mike made saddles during his off hours whenever he could. He completed his first custom saddle in 1978, while working at Deseret. It sold for $350, less than the cost of a saddle tree today, and made a small profit. He set up shop in his new home and worked during the day in order to provide for his family as his saddle-making business grew. During 1991–92, he had a shop in Eli's Western Wear in Okeechobee. Business

Mike Wilder, a saddle maker. *Florida Archives.*

was good. "I had more work than three men could do," he recalled. But he ultimately tired of working in a confined space and commuting ninety miles a day. He moved his shop into the barn at his home, where he continues to make custom saddles today.

Most of the saddles Mike makes are "unadorned tools of the trade" used by working cowboys. Over the years, he has earned a reputation for building rugged, finely crafted, comfortable saddles that will last a lifetime. He is skilled at leather carving (or "hand-tooling," as some say) and credits renowned leather carver Bob Dellis for showing him some of the finer points of the craft when he lived in Okeechobee. But Mike usually limits his ornamentation to a small amount of border or basket-weave stamping. "Decoration and carving is not what people come to me for," he stated in his typically modest manner.

The first step in building a custom saddle is to meet with the client and discuss their needs and preferences. Often, Mike will examine the client's horse and take some measurements, especially if the animal has a history of being difficult to comfortably fit to a saddle. Mike uses only the finest materials throughout. The rawhide-covered tree is the foundation of the saddle, and Mike has been buying top-quality trees from Timberline Saddle Tree Inc. of Vernal, Utah, for decades. He purchases his leather from Wickett and Craig in Curwensville, Pennsylvania, which was established in 1867. All the metal hardware he uses is of the highest quality.

As is the case with most saddle-makers, Mike probably spends about half his time doing repair work. One benefit of doing repairs is that he learns what the weak points of various saddles are and how to avoid those faults. Consequently, his saddles have become increasingly durable over time.

In addition to making and repairing saddles, Mike is often asked to craft custom leather goods—hand-carved electric guitar covers, notebooks, fancy chaps, saddle bags and gun holsters, you name it. Because Mike's craftsmanship is appreciated and respected by his peers, he is often called on to furnish special items for ranching community events. For years, he made the award saddle for the all-around cowboy at Silver Spurs. He made special commemorative saddles for the Great Florida Cattle Drives of 1995, 2006, 2016 and 2022. In his service as cow boss for the 2006, 2016 and 2022 events, he was responsible for the welfare and movement of more than five hundred head of cattle during the week-long event.

Mike has twice been recognized by the Florida Department of State. In 1995, he served as a master artist, teaching Greg Gaughan saddle-making under the Florida Folk Arts Apprenticeship Program. In 2008, the secretary of state honored him with the Florida Folk Heritage Award in recognition of his excellence in hand-crafting saddles for the ranching community. He figures he has made over five hundred custom saddles, and there is no sign that he will be slowing down anytime soon.

## *Spurs*
## *Billy Davis*

Billy Davis has spent a lifetime working with cattle in Florida and is acknowledged by his peers as an expert cowman. "You've got to read the cow," declared Billy. "She'll tell you what she needs. I feel blessed to be able to read a cow like I can because of my ancestors. It's like respect. You don't just get it. You've got to work for it."

Billy's family history of raising cattle in Florida began in the early nineteenth century. His paternal great-great-great-great-grandfather William Davis (1790–1860) came from North Carolina, and after spending some time in Georgia, he decided to settle in present-day Polk County, Florida, in 1824. Several of Billy's ancestors on both sides of his family fought in the Seminole Wars and the Civil War. Billy's grandfather Luther Davis (1888–1962) was born in Fort Meade and, in 1910, married Sophia Prescott (1894–1982). Luther Davis was a cattle owner, cowboy and horse trader. "They say he traded a blind mule for two two-year-old horses," Billy remarked with a chuckle.

Billy's father, Earl D. Davis (1920–1986), the fourth of Luther and Sophie's five children, was born in Hardee County. Billy's mother, Vera Simmons Davis (1923–2016), was born in Pompano Beach and died in Okeechobee. As far as Billy knows, all the male members of his family who lived in Florida raised cattle or worked for those who did.

William "Billy" D. Davis, the youngest of five children, was born in St. Augustine in 1953. He left home when he was sixteen and moved to the Kenansville area to break horses for Buck Lee, a local cattleman who also owned the community store. Next, he went to work breaking horses for the Adams Ranch at nearby Lake Marion. "I was riding up to seven colts a day, making sixty dollars a week and living by myself," he recalled. "I tried rodeoing on the weekends, but that career didn't last too long," he continued. "I rode saddle horses and a few bulls. I probably spent $10,000 and won about $300."

Eventually, he returned to Okeechobee, where he worked as a day rider (he does not care for the term *day worker*) and broke horses. Billy married Cynthia Shaw in 1973. They have three daughters, Sommer Lea, Jennifer Lea, Billie Dee, and two grandchildren.

Having spent a lifetime working outdoors, Billy has plenty of experience with lightning. He vividly recalls working with his father and a crew on the Radebaugh Ranch in the 1970s. "It came up a hell of a storm, lightning was popping everywhere. Daddy said, 'Boys, if you'll pay attention, you will see something that you won't see again in your life.' With that static electricity, there wasn't a breath of air nowhere. Them cattle would touch and could see that blue spark coming off 'em just a-crackling."

Billy Davis making spurs. *Florida Archives.*

Billy is a firm believer in the utility of cow dogs and enjoys a reputation for having well-trained dogs that are effective workers. "It's just the most satisfying thing to me when I hear that dog and lope on over there and see he's got that bunch of cattle held up." He controls his dogs with three signals to go, stay or get water. "I don't let my dogs just go to them water holes, especially when it's dry, because there may be a gator in there." Billy usually works with two grown dogs and a puppy that is learning to work by imitating the older dogs. Currently, he has nine cow dogs, four at home and five that he keeps at the ranch.

Billy was among the founders of the Florida Cracker Horse Association in 1989 and has served as its president in the past. "I've rode Cracker horses all my life," stated Billy.

> *I get along with them. They don't have no quit in 'em. The other horses I've rode—quarter horses mainly—they have a limit to them. You can bust one's heart pretty quick. I'm rough on horses and found out at an early age that Cracker horses would stand up underneath me. I do all my cow pen work on horseback. It keeps the cattle calmer, and my Cracker horse is so little that he don't intimidate cattle. I'll have a crowding pen full of cattle, and I can get right in there on my Cracker horse and sort that cow out. You get a big horse in there, and to start with, there ain't enough room for him to get around in there. If it's a concrete pen and muddy, he's going to slip down with you 'cause he really don't give a damn if he hurts his self or not.*
>
> *That little Cracker horse will take care of his self; therefore, he is taking care of you. Sometimes, when I'm in that crowding pen, parting cows and calves on that concrete, I sling mud and cow manure everywhere. But my Cracker horse has got all four feet right there on that concrete. He don't ever slip.*

While some would argue that you can't rope a bull from a Cracker horse, Billy has done it many times. "Every year, I'll have to rope one or two bulls, and my horse don't weigh but 850 pounds with a heavy saddle on it. You've just got to know what you are doing. You can't just dash out there and rope a two-thousand-pound bull."

Some cowmen are quick to get rid of an uncooperative cow that requires roping, but that's a practice Billy disagrees with. "You've got to read that cow. It's not just an object and a way to make money. If she's a three-year-old cow and wants to give me trouble but she has a six-hundred-pound calf, no, I'm not going to rope her and choke her either. I'll take my time and take care of her."

In 2008, Billy was asked to work for the Pressley Ranch on State Road 60, a few miles west of Vero Beach. "I wanted that job all my life," he declared. "They respect me as much as I respect them." The Pressley Ranch herd comprises about one thousand mother cows. "I raise some dang good calves," he proudly stated. "The highest weight of my seven to ten month

Billy Davis riding Cracker horse "Little Richard." *Florida Archives.*

olds was 618 pounds." Pressley Ranch retains ownership of their calves in the feedlot until they reach 1,100 to 1,300 pounds.

When not busy working at the Pressley Ranch, Billy can usually be found in the shop at his home, crafting custom spurs. "Whatever needs to be done at the ranch always comes first," he firmly stated. He has had a lifelong fascination with spurs. "I've always been amazed with spurs, even when I was a little feller. I turned a teenager and boy, I'd buy me a pair of spurs and wear 'em for a couple or three weeks, and then I'd see another pair that I just had to have, so I'd get them. They just fascinated me, you know, for some reason." Billy has collected antique spurs and bits for years and generously loaned several artifacts to the Florida Cattlemen's Foundation's Museum exhibit *Five Centuries of Tradition*.

Once his three daughters were raised and his work schedule permitted, he began making spurs. "I started trying to build spurs about 1993, and in 1995, [I] went to Amarillo, Texas, to study spur-making with Jerry Cates, focusing on silver work." Today, Billy finely crafts utilitarian custom spurs, that are handsome and will last for years under the toughest conditions. His spur-making business has steadily grown, and he has a backlog of orders. As a lifelong working cowboy, Billy knows what his clients—mostly people from his region—want and what their budgets will allow. He provides spurs that fulfill their needs.

Acutely aware of the encroachment of residential development in cattle country, Billy Davis considers himself fortunate to have worked on several of Florida's large ranches, many of which are no longer in operation. His generation may be the last to routinely work cattle on large expanses of rough, wild country. He enjoys the satisfaction of raising quality calves on the Pressley Ranch, making high-quality spurs and spending time with his family.

## Cow Whips
## Junior Mills

The cow whip is an essential part of working cowboy gear and an icon of Florida cattle ranching. Florida cowmen use long, braided leather whips to control the movement of cattle, though the whips seldom touch the animals. The cattle respond to the loud *crack* of the whip without having to be struck.

In Okeechobee, Florida, cow hunter George "Junior" Mills painstakingly fashioned whips from buckskin by first cutting the strings from tanned leather hides and then plaiting several layers in a carefully controlled taper. To achieve a smooth taper, the dimensions to which he cut the strings had to be exact. Then he carefully plaited them under just the right amount of tension. The "belly," or the thickest part, of the whips consisted of four layers. At the end of the whips, he tied a thin piece of deerskin about a foot long called a "Cracker." It was this component that was responsible for the loud noise the whips produced. He protected his finish from sun, sand and

Junior Mills making cow whips with his apprentice Buddy Mills. *Florida Archives.*

abrasion by coating them with a mixture he made by heating beef tallow, beeswax and pine rosin. Junior mentored his son Calvin "Buddy" Mills, who handcrafted his first buckskin cow whip at the age of fifteen.

Today, Florida cowboys use rodent and weatherproof whips plaited from braided nylon cord. The Florida cow whip is fastened to a wooden handle by two thongs, a distinctive feature that gives them more flexibility than whips plaited over the handle.

## KEEPING FLORIDA'S RANCHING HISTORY ALIVE

The State of Florida recently celebrated five hundred years of ranching history, acknowledging the part that Spanish heritage horses and cattle played in shaping the industry that changed the course of history in North America. Florida also celebrated the ranchers who steward millions of acres of ranchland. This was accomplished and continues to be accomplished through the efforts of many groups on several different fronts.

### *Ranchland Preservation*

Florida is a national leader in land protection and has two state land protection programs that protect its ranchlands: Florida Forever and the Rural and Family Lands Protection Program. These programs purchase conservation easements over ranchlands and protect the properties from development in perpetuity. Iconic ranching landscapes highlight a part of Florida's history and heritage that goes beyond the beaches. Few people get to see or experience these landscapes, but millions of us rely on them. These ranches feed people and provide vital flood control, temporarily storing floodwaters in times of disasters caused by hurricanes, acting as a rural sponge by soaking up excess water that would otherwise be permanently lost.

During the last trying two years of an epidemic that brought to a halt much of our nation's economy and the daily flow of our lives, farmers and ranchers—who could never take a day off—worked to keep Florida's people fed. With Florida's population growing rapidly, preserving and protecting more of its rural lands and waters provides not only vital habitat for wide-ranging wildlife but also aids in groundwater recharge that provides drinking water to Floridians and visitors across the state.

Several important environmental action groups have recently gained momentum to carry the promise of preserving our ranch lands while at the same time preserving the habitats of many species of animals, critical sources of water and scenic landscapes. Since its founding in 1999, Conservancy Florida has led the way in land protection and has saved over thirty thousand acres of critical habitat through conservation projects, now actively working on over one hundred thousand acres. The agency saves land by developing conservation strategies, exploring funding sources and accepting land donations and conservation easements, helping guide landowners through the land protection process and promoting land conservation through effective education and advocacy.

Conservation easements are the most secure tools available to landowners to protect rural land. They are perpetual restrictions on subdivision development and other land uses, and they are tailored to the agricultural, forestry, recreational and ecologic goals of the landowner. The future of ranching in Florida depends on both the next generation of ranchers and the will of the people of Florida and their leaders to preserve this way of life through conservation easements and efforts like the Florida Wildlife Corridor Program.

In 2021, Florida witnessed the monumental bipartisan passing of the Florida Wildlife Corridor Act that supports legislative findings that the state's population is growing rapidly and that lands and waters that provide the state's green infrastructure and vital habitats for wide-ranging wildlife, such as the Florida panther, need to be preserved and protected. The Wildlife Corridor is a network of connected wildlife habitats that are required for the long-term survival of and genetic exchange among regional wildlife populations that serve to prevent fragmentation by providing connectivity of the lands needed to furnish adequate habitats and allow safe movement of wildlife as well as flood and sea level rise resiliency. This act officially recognizes the ecological value of nearly twenty million acres of land in Florida, including land currently used for forestry, farming and cattle ranching, and provides incentive to help safeguard it.

Legacy Ranches are historic ranches within Florida's iconic Wildlife Corridor that preserve natural habitats, as well as farming and ranching infrastructure that

A Florida panther. *Florida Archives.*

An aerial
photograph of
Adams Ranch.
*Adams Ranch.*

is the foundation of the state's economy. Some of these ranches are already under conservation easements. Treasure Hammock Ranch in Indian River County was the first property in the state of Florida to receive a conservation easement designed primarily to protect agriculture. Adams Ranch in Okeechobee County has received numerous environmental awards, including the Ranch of the Century Award from the National Cattlemen's Association, and has been placed under a conservation easement. The Williamson Cattle Company of Okeechobee County was the first ranch east of the Mississippi to receive the National Environmental Stewardship Award from the National Cattlemen's Association.

## CEREMONIAL TRAIL RIDES AND CATTLE DRIVES

### *Ridin' the Florida Cracker Trail*

On a chilly Monday morning, February 20, 2010, as a gentle breeze wafted through miles of open pasture on Duck Smith's Bar Crescent S Ranch in Wauchula, the twenty-third annual Florida Cracker Trail Association ride got underway. On Friday, February 19, registration began at the Kible Ranch, with more than 150 riders signed up for five days of camping, entertainment and camaraderie to the trail's end in Fort Pierce.

The Florida Cracker Trail Association includes experienced and not-so-experienced riders who want to trek the legendary 1800s cattle trail that cow hunters used to herd thousands of head of cattle, destined for shipment north of Fort Pierce and Punta Rassa, south of Fort Myers, to market, where cow hunters loaded herds onto paddleboats bound for Cuba to replenish the beef supply after the Spanish-American War in 1898.

After two days at the Bar Crescent S Ranch that included three hearty meals a day served from Pat's Barbecue Chuck Wagon of Lake Placid, the last night was filled with music by "Cracker Tenor" Benjamin Dehart. For me, riding a beautiful palomino on loan from Mark Roberts of Duck Smith's Bar S Ranch, the living heritage of the cow hunters came alive.

Duck Smith led riders through his property, stopping for a lunch break before moving toward the next camp by the Peace River. There were wagons pulled by draft ponies and a cavalry of mustangs, Cracker horses, paints and mounts and riders dressed in traditional plaid shirts, scarves and colorful chaps, reliving those by-gone days. Horses were rigged with lariats, Cracker whips and tack used in the old days.

On the first Friday night, the Cracker Trail Association inducted Pershing Platt of Zolpho Springs into the 2010 Cracker Hall of Fame. When Platt was sixteen years old, he drove his family's cattle across Florida from Melbourne to Horse Creek in Hardee County and on to Ona. At sixty-eight, Platt saddled up again to ride the Florida Cracker Trail, then designated as the official Cracker Trail. At the time of his induction, Platt was ninety years old.

The Cracker Trail caravan was escorted by Hardee County sheriff's deputies and stopped at Zolpho Springs Elementary School to let students pet the horses. Then it traveled over twenty miles to the Putnam Ranch. On Thursday, the riders left Ashton Ranch and moved to the Pearce Estate along the Kissimmee River, meandering through scrub country to the Bass Ranch. The last trek was nineteen miles to the Adams Ranch in Fort Pierce.

With great fanfare on Saturday, the Cracker Trail riders reached Fort Pierce and paraded through town to the Backus Museum and Gallery on the Intracoastal Waterway, escorted by the Fort Pierce Police and St. Lucie County sheriff's deputies. The streets were lined with spectators, who rushed up to the horses to catch treats the trail riders threw. At trail's end, there was a Cracker cow campsite, blacksmith demonstration, swamp cabbage tasting and music by the Green River Band. It was an eclectic event that brought life to the legendary history and culture of Florida's pioneer cow hunters, as shared by author Nancy Dale in *The Legacy of the Florida Pioneer Cow Hunters*.

# THE HISTORY OF THE GREAT FLORIDA CATTLE DRIVES
## BY DOYLE CONNER JR.

In 1995, Floridians celebrated the 150th birthday of our state with a year's worth of festivities. The Florida Cracker Cattle Association began thinking about how to use the occasion to shine a light on the history, culture and traditions of Florida's cattle families. After a lot of discussion, it was decided that the Florida Cracker Cattle Association would push ahead to make it happen. Then they pointed at me and said, "You are the chairman." The thought of assuming the responsibility of such a project was a bit scary, but we charged ahead when everyone in the room agreed to be on the committee.

In early 1993, we began having monthly meetings in Kissimmee. We asked anyone interested in planning, promoting and producing this adventure to just to show up. I guess I was the luckiest man in the world, because the room filled up with talented, strong and committed people from all walks of life and all parts of the state. Some of them had notable names among Florida cow folk, like Tucker, Yarborough, Bass, Overstreet, Lykes, Whaley and Bronson.

It was decided that we would drive one thousand head of cattle for about a week over some of our best and most historic ranchland in Osceola County. We wanted to invite anyone and everyone to join us on the trail, as long as they could rough it like cow hunters, dress like old timers and be prepared for whatever nature and the Lord sent our way. In order to raise one thousand head of cattle, we told each of the County Cattlemen's Associations that if they would find and donate at least twenty head of Cracker/Spanish-type cattle, we would allow them to send their designated county cow hunter and a county wagon for free. We told many ranchers that they, too, could join us if they brought twenty head or more to the herd.

We asked some friends who were members of the Seminole tribe of Florida to partner with us. I knew that for almost one hundred years, the Seminoles had been "the keepers of the cattle" in Florida, and I am pleased to say the tribe jumped in and were a very integral part of our efforts. We also reached out to other businesses and found amazing support from the Florida Cattlemen's Association, the Florida Department of Agriculture and Consumer Services, Seminole Feeds, Dodge Trucks of Central Florida and the Kissimmee and St. Cloud TDC. Thanks to these great folks, we raise almost $200,000, which helped promote and advertise the drive and defer some of the costs of registration fees.

So, what finally happened in 1995? We drove one thousand head of cattle from Adams Blanket Bay down State Road 60, into the Silver Spurs Arena. We drove them across some of Florida's most historic ranches and through some of the Sunshine State's most beautiful territory. We trailed six hundred horses and riders and forty or so wagons. We had historic reenactors from some important stage of Florida's history at each camp and literally "rode through time." We had a huge frolic and trade fair at the Spurs Arena, with hundreds of "period singers," along with artists and craftsmen who showcased their skills. And we had an amazing musical finale, which included the Bellamy Brothers, along with Seminole chief James Billy, cowboy poets and the cow hunters themselves, who drove the cattle into the arena and went into a "mill" like the cattle stampedes of old.

Our goal was to have a good time and share Florida's cow culture and traditions with the world. We were overwhelmingly successful. We had front-page coverage in newspapers in Tokyo, Melbourne, London, Paris, Belgrade, San Paulo, Toronto and all over the United States. Millions of people from around the world now know that the cattle ranching industry began in Florida with the first horses and cattle brought by the Spanish in 1521. We have held a ceremonial cattle drive about every ten years since, joined by such influential people such as Governor Lawton Childs and Commissioners of Agriculture Adam Putnam and Nikki Fried. And some participants rode Cracker horses, descendants of those first horses, and drove Cracker cattle, descendants of those first cattle, Florida's heritage animals, alive and well after five hundred years.

The most recent drive, held in December 2022, commemorated five hundred years of cattle and horse production in Florida; 350 riders and horses, 14 wagons and 1 pedestrian pushed 1,500 cattle (three different groups) through eighty miles of the most pristine ranches on the planet. We will forever be grateful to the Kirchman Foundation Lake X Ranch, the Deseret Ranch (one of the largest ranches in America, covering almost three hundred thousand acres), the Kempfer Ranch, the Escape Ranch, the Diego Mandina Ranch and the Three Lakes Wildlife Management Area for sharing with us the beauty of their holdings. The logistics of moving a large group through the wilds of our state can be compared only to a military operation.

Participants, known as cow hunters, slept on the ground, slogged through the wet, choked down the dust and cussed the fireweed. Crackers, Yankees, Seminoles, city folk and country folk from Canada to South America wanted to taste the life of our cow hunting ancestors. For seven days and nights, people of every color and creed learned to work together and respect the difficulties the old timers faced every day of their lives.

People did the drive for many different reasons—for the adventure of being out in nature for a week, to future condition their horse and themselves, to make a spiritual pilgrimage to heal or make amends or simply to be a part of a large community of like-minded people. One gentleman walked the entire drive in 2016 in memory of his wife who had recently passed away. For whatever reason, most people were ready to start over again when the drive ended, savoring the sense of exhilaration and satisfaction for having pushed themselves beyond normal their limits.

## *Lindy's Story*

One of my trail-riding friends told me of her experience doing the cattle drive previously, and I made plans with several friends. But I made up my mind that I was going do it whether I knew anyone or not. I prepared for months. Not having primitively camped in many years, I tested out a couple tents, had a blast looking for "authentic" pioneer clothing, read *A Land Remembered*, by Patrick Smith and, of course, rode daily to get myself and my horse in shape for the challenge.

It was magical from the beginning. Everyone was so welcoming and friendly. When I arrived the first day, before the drive started, I rode around the camp meeting people, learning of their journey that brought them to the event, hearing about the horse they were riding and getting my horse used to the environment of so many horses, wagons, mules and people. It was exciting to see others getting into period dress as well, and the magic continued as we took off the first morning.

The drive was divided into six different circles, each identified by a specific colored bandanna that participants received when they arrived. Each circle camped together at night and had two trailer drivers who moved the camping gear and horse feed to the next camp each morning. Our circle boss was "Cracker" Jack Gillen, a native Floridian who raises Cracker cattle and horses and is a veteran of all four cattle drives, and "Mama Jack," his wife, drove our trailer and acted as our "cattle drive concierge." Our chuckwagon boss was Jed Mitchell's Catering. He and his crew were over the top! We ate meals our ancestors could only dream about—steak, barbecued pork, fettuccini alfredo with grilled chicken and a variety of wonderful sides and deserts. It's amazing that he could cook for that many people after moving

Lindy and "Sedona," GFCD 2022. *Lindy Kandoza.*

his crew and equipment each day—breakfast at 7:00 a.m., dinner at 7:00 p.m. and a packed lunch we grabbed at breakfast each day.

Different circles rotated riding at the front with the herd with the cow crew and dogs. Our circle was able to drive the cattle the first and the longest day in the saddle, and it was so exciting. My horse "Sedona" took to it right away, guiding the cattle back to their herd when they strayed. Sharing this experience with others was fabulous!

Riding all day without a building in sight on such beautiful ranches was a dream come true and simply breathtaking. I took advantage of being able to lope through the fields and explore the canopies of live oaks. If there was a hill, we climbed it, or a ditch or pond, we rode through it. I wanted the full cowgirl experience, and I got it!

Watching the real wranglers and their dogs handle the stampedes and runaways gave me a real appreciation for how hard they work, as well as the abilities of their horses and dogs. I admire their grit, as well as their kindness when things did not go as expected.

## Kevin's Story

I went on the ride with my ten-year-old granddaughter, Emma Smith. Due to some bad choices on the part of her parents, my wife and I adopted Emma when she was two years old. About three years ago, Emma became interested in horses, and after a few false starts, we ended up with a quarter horse named Oreo, who became Emma's "heart horse." Emma does barrels and poles and light trail riding. We also adopted a Bureau of Land Management Mustang in April 2021.

Because I wanted to have an experience with Emma that we would both treasure for years to come, I reached out to Lynn Yarborough, who was on the Great Florida Cattle Drive Committee, for advice. She assured us that with some preparation ahead of time, we would be able to do it and that both Emma and I would be fine, and we were.

Emma and I bonded even more, working hand in hand, setting up and tearing down camp each day. The days were filled with laughter and joy, and we had never had so much fun. We learned more about Florida history and developed so many friendships. "Oreo" and "Kevin", our mustang, just ten months fresh from Nevada (he came with that name—guess it was a good sign) both did great. I learned more about horses and life in general than I could ever have dreamed of.

I had tears of joy when we rode into the arena on the last day. I was so proud we made it. I felt so blessed to see my wife, daughter and granddaughter cheering us on. And I will forever be grateful to Lynn for easing my anxiety and giving me the courage to make the memories.

## Emma's Story

The Great Florida Cattle Drive was so much fun! My horse "Oreo" couldn't have been any better. "Oreo" and I loved going through the water, and sometimes, the cattle swam with us. The cow crew was especially helpful, because sometimes, when the cattle stampeded, they had to go out and round them all back up.

At the end of each day, I would look for our night camp and trot over to our circle's trailer and grab our supplies and start setting

Emma Smith taking a break, GFCD 2022. *Kevin Smith.*

up camp and the corral for our horses. Papa would get there eventually, but I always had our campsite picked out and started the work of setting up.

The activities were always different each night. I loved dancing around the fire with the Seminoles and my new friends. But I did not like the dew each morning that made everything so wet. I would do it all over again if I could do it with my papa.

## Sonnie's Story

This trip was one I will cherish for the rest of my days. I will never forget joining such an awesome group of people on such a historic ride. Most of all, I will never forget the kindness and love shown to my grandson, Declan, who was given the nickname "Paco" by his cattle drive friends. I am very grateful to all who took him in and gave him solid cowboy advice and helped him thrive in an environment that brought him so much joy. We had an awesome circle boss, Domingo Hernandez, and his kindness will always be treasured.

Moving the Cracker cattle on the last day was the most memorable part of the drive for me, because it felt like the real deal as we pushed them through the pines, palmettos and swamps and as we drove the cattle, I imagined what it must have been like in the early days. I realized the hardships we experienced on the drive were nothing compared to the ones experienced by our ancestors. Knowing this made it all that much more of an honor to be a part of this event.

I can't imagine what it must have been like organizing this event, but I am sure thankful to those who stepped up and took the time and effort to do it. See y'all on the reunion ride!

## "Paco" Declan's Story

Declan "Paco," GFCD 2022.
*Sonnie Graham.*

I got the opportunity of a lifetime to go on the Great Florida Cattle Drive with my seventy-year-old granddaddy, Sonnie Graham. I was just a few days shy of my ninth birthday, and what a great birthday present it was. We knew people who had gone on the drive before, and we couldn't resist the opportunity for such a cool adventure. I switched off with my granddaddy riding "Red," an American quarter horse, and "Fancy," an American paint horse.

I made lots of friends, mostly chatting my way through the camp while my granddaddy was making and breaking our camp. The friends I made in our circle made me feel like a real member of our crew. All of them were so kind, even if we didn't speak the same language. They shared lots of snacks with me, lots of good advice and even a black cowboy hat! I had the most awesome circle boss turned friend, Mr. Domingo Hernandez.

I had the time of my life. I just can't explain how much fun it was. One of my favorite parts was driving the cows and riding my way through any water in my path (even if I had to make it a part of my path). It was just too hard to resist.

Being able to go with my granddaddy (one of my favorite people on Earth) on such a special trip is something I'll never forget. Thank you to everyone for all the hard work that it took to make this possible. Y'all ain't no sissies! See ya on the trail!

## Richelle's Story

Richelle Rowley riding "Sage," GFCD 2022. *Author's collection.*

Richelle Rowley got her horse "Sage" from a children's home of all places. He was misbehaving, and they begged her to take him. After Richelle broke him of his bad habits, she decided to ride him on the cattle drive. "He was a 'star attraction' the minute he got with the herd," she said. "He knew exactly what to do, and everyone, especially the cow crew, noticed. I just let him do what came naturally and tried to keep up," she said, beaming from ear to ear. "All the old cow hunters told me what a good job we did! I never knew where he came from originally, but it is obvious he knows how to herd cattle." She shared that her seventeen-year-old son and his best friend had recently been killed by a drunk driver, and she was reminded that tomorrow is not promised to anyone. She was extremely happy she took time out to experience the healing powers of nature and to be with people who loved to ride horses and recreate a piece of Florida's history.

Happy trails to you—until we meet again...

*Above*: Jennifer Schuck riding "Ricki," GFCD 2022. "Honestly, I would never trade this experience for an all-inclusive resort ever. I love the adventure and the challenge. I really loved that the organizers encouraged our military veterans and Sheriff's Boys Ranch to participate. Passing on the legacy of the working cowboy in Florida is crucial to our survival. I literally never stopped smiling the entire drive." *Author's collection.*

*Left*: Amanda Carpenter, a veteran rider and trainer, riding "Too Pretty" (from Payne Midyette's Cracker stud "Pretty Boy" and Celina Murray's Cracker mare "Sally Too") GFCD 2022. *Author's collection.*

*Above*: Wendy Wilson (*left*), with Florida cowgirl friends Kara Rhoden, Rebecca Hurm, Katie Rhoden and Sarah Ewald, reflects, "The energy of having over three hundred horses around you, riding through this beautiful land was intense. A stampede can be terrifying, and you depend on your instincts and horse to take care of you. What it takes to put dinner on the table is something many don't understand, and experiencing this drive gave me a greater appreciation for what ranchers do for us." *Author's collection.*

*Right*: Haley Naramore with Cracker horse "Bella" GFCD 2022. *Author's collection.*

*Top*: John Howard riding "Little Man" (Ayers herd), Sharon Moore riding "Lucky" (Ayers/ Trasher herd), Karen Howard riding "Little Bit" (Ayers herd) and Elena Carpenter riding "Lady" GFCD 2022. *Author's collection.*

*Middle*: Crystal Blevins riding Cracker horse "Chico" GFCD 2022. *Author's collection.*

*Bottom*: Jack Gillen, Martha Ackeroyd (the blue circle flag bearer) and M.B. bringing home the herd GFCD 2022. *Author's collection.*

*Top*: Driving home the herd GFCD 2022. *Author's collection.*

*Bottom*: Cowhunters, "buckskin circle." GFCD 2022. *Domingo Hernandez .*

# BIBLIOGRAPHY

Akerman, Joe, Jr. *Florida Cattle Frontier: Over 400 Years of Cattle Raising.* Kissimmee: Florida Cattlemen's Association and the Florida Cracker Cattle Association, 2003.

————. *Florida Cowman: A History of Florida Cattle Raising.* Kissimmee: Florida Cattlemen's Association, 1976.

Bennett, Deb, PhD. *Conquerors: The Roots of New World Horsemanship.* Los Angeles, CA: Amigo Publications Inc., 1998.

Crary, Rick. "Florida Cowman, Bud Adams." *Indian River Magazine*, 2007.

Dale, Nancy. *The Legacy of the Florida Pioneer Cow Hunters.* Bloomington, IN: IUniverse, 2011.

*Florida Cattle Ranching: Five Centuries of Tradition.* Kissimmee: Florida Cattlemen's Association, 2013.

Getzen, Sam. "The Florida Cracker Heritage Horse." *Florida Cracker Horse Association Newsletter.*

"Legacy Ranches: A Way of Life Worth Preserving; Conserving Agriculture Land for the Future of Florida; the Momentum of the Wildlife Corridor Coalition." Essays in Florida Ranches Calendar 2022. Stacy Ramieri, dir. Palm Beach, FL: Firefly Group.

Ste. Claire, Dana. *Cracker: Cracker Culture in Florida History.* Gainesville: University Press of Florida, 2006.

Tinsley, Jim Bob. *Florida Cow Hunter: The Life and Times of Bone Mizell.* Gainesville: University Press of Florida, 1991.

Ward, Carlton, Jr. *Florida Cowboys: Keepers of the Last Frontier.* Gainesville: University Press of Florida, 2009.

# ABOUT THE AUTHOR

**C**arol Matthews taught elementary school for forty years. A graduate of Ohio University, her love of history began at an early age, when she would search for arrowheads after the annual spring plowing of her father's cornfields. The last seventeen years of her teaching career were spent in a small agricultural town in Florida called Indiantown in western Martin County, where she discovered an unlikely history mentor in the form of a spunky cattle rancher, well known as simply Miss Iris in her circle throughout the state. Carol was Martin County's Teacher of the Year in 2008 and is a member of the Florida Cracker Horse and Cracker Cattle Associations. *Cracker Horses and Cattle: A History of Florida's Heritage Breeds* is her third book on Florida history. You may contact her at 772-284-8202 for more information.